48-Hour Makeovers

Editor: Brian Kramer

Senior Associate Design Director: Ken Carlson

Project Editor and Writer: Jan Soults Walker

Contributing Editor: Amy Tincher-Durik

Contributing Art Directors: Chris Conyers, Chad Johnston, Beth Runcie, Joe Wysong, Conyers Design, Inc.

Contributing Writers: Amber D. Barz, Kellie Kramer

Contributing Project Designers: Carrie Hansen; Rebecca Jerdee; Cathy Kramer, Cathy Kramer Designs

Contributing Photographers: William Hopkins, Scott Little, William Stites, Rick Taylor, Paul Whicheloe (Anyway Productions Inc.)

Illustrator: Michael Burns

Copy Chief: Terri Fredrickson

Copy and Production Editor: Victoria Forlini

Editorial Operations Manager: Karen Schirm

Managers, Book Production: Pam Kvitne, Marjorie J. Schenkelberg, Rick von Holdt, Mark Weaver

Contributing Copy Editor: Jane Woychick

Contributing Proofreaders: Sue Fetters, Heidi Johnson, Brenda Scott Royce

Indexer: Beverly A. Nightenhelser

Editorial and Design Assistants: Kaye Chabot, Karen McFadden, Mary Lee Gavin

Meredith₀ Books
Editor in Chief: Linda Raglan Cunningham
Design Director: Matt Strelecki
Executive Editor, Home Decorating and Design: Denise L. Caringer

Publisher: James D. Blume
Executive Director, Marketing: Jeffrey Myers
Executive Director, New Business Development: Todd M. Davis
Executive Director, Sales: Ken Zagor
Director, Operations: George A. Susral
Director, Production: Douglas M. Johnston
Business Director: Jim Leonard

Vice President and General Manager: Douglas J. Guendel

Meredith Publishing Group
President, Publishing Group: Stephen M. Lacy
Vice President-Publishing Director: Bob Mate

Meredith Corporation
Chairman and Chief Executive Officer: William T. Kerr

In Memoriam: E. T. Meredith III (1933–2003)

TLC (The Learning Channel), TLC (The Learning Channel) logo, *Trading Spaces*, and the *Trading Spaces* logo are trademarks of Discovery Communications, Inc., used under license.

The decorating projects and how-to instructions set forth in this book are not necessarily endorsed or recommended by the *Trading Spaces* designers and are intended instead to illustrate some of the basic techniques that can be used in home decorating.

***Trading Spaces* Book Development Team**
Kathy Davidov, Executive Producer, TLC
Roger Marmet, General Manager, TLC
Tom Farrell, Executive Producer, Banyan Productions
Sharon M. Bennett, Senior Vice President, Strategic Partnerships & Licensing
Carol LeBlanc, Vice President, Marketing, Strategic Partnerships
Erica Jacobs Green, Publishing Manager
Elizabeth Bakacs, Creative Director, Strategic Partnerships

Trading Spaces

48-Hour Makeovers

Meredith® Books
Des Moines, Iowa

contents

tick... tick... tick...

it's time for a

If that hummable theme song is the flashy musical riff of *Trading Spaces*, then the ticking of the countdown clock is the steady backbeat for each decorating makeover.

Watch a few episodes of *Trading Spaces* and you'll probably realize that one constant, ever-present element exists in every episode. No, not host Paige Davis! The steadfast commodity of the *Trading Spaces* experience is time.

In the world of *Trading Spaces,* time is a fixed resource: Designers can't pick up an extra gallon of it at the home center. Paige memorably summed up the hard truth about time during Designer Chat in San Diego: Duenda Road when she said, "You can't spend money to buy time."

Designers have some flexibility regarding money restrictions on the show (they *can* choose to go over budget and literally pay the consequences); however, they cannot exceed the time limit. At the end of Day 2, before the *Trading Spaces* crew moves on to a completely new location, the finished (or partially finished) designs must be revealed to homeowners and viewers alike.

Having only 48 hours to complete a makeover isn't necessarily a negative—on the show or in your own decorating projects. Have

you ever been trapped in a never-ending room redo—you know, the kind of decorating project that goes on for weeks or months? Concentrating your efforts and committing to a 48-hour time frame lets you move full steam ahead toward a complete makeover—all in a weekend.

When you're making over a space in a limited amount of time, free yourself up to choose, to move, to groove—to go with the moment. Sure, like some of the homeowners on the show, you may decide to go back and rework a design later or finish up some details; however, for 48 hours you'll focus entirely on completing the bulk of the transformation fast and *now*.

On the show and in real life, planning and preparation are the keys to getting major decorating results in limited time. *Trading Spaces 48-Hour Makeovers* gives you indispensable information for transforming any space in a mere 48 hours.

change

▶PART I: THE MAKEOVER METHOD
gives you everything you need to dream up, plan, and execute your own makeover.

▶PART II: MAKEOVERS IN MOTION
provides an up-close look at 14 fabulous room makeovers featured on *Trading Spaces* and *Trading Spaces Family.* You'll find out how the designers and homeowners pulled off each of these amazing transformations in only two days' time.

"Fast Project Inspired by the Show" features all the steps, materials, and skills you need to complete 14 supercool decorating projects yourself in mere minutes.

"From the Designers" sidebars offer exclusive timesaving strategies from the *Trading Spaces* cast.

▶PART III: ROOM ARRANGING KIT
gives you an easy-to-use kit and loads of tips on how to arrange furniture and accessories for maximum design impact.

With sidebars, tips, and *Trading Spaces* humor, *Trading Spaces 48-Hour Makeovers* is your guide to rapid, room-changing design. Block out a weekend or take a few days of vacation; the time for a new look is now. Get reading, get dreaming, and get ready to go!

timely thoughts

Who knew that the *Trading Spaces* crew could be so wise and witty on the topic of time? Here are some favorite tidbits from the show:

▶ **"Can I just, like, blink and click my heels, and this'll be done?"**
—*Laurie in New Jersey: Tall Pines Drive*

▶ **"I wish you spent as much time laying this project out as you did on your hair this morning."**
—*One of Doug's homeowners addressing Doug during Washington, D.C.: Cleveland Park*

▶ **"Precision doesn't have to go overtime; you just have to be well-planned."**
—*Vern in Maryland: Fairway Court*

▶ **"Time is money?! Let me write that down so I can embroider that on a whoopee cushion."**
—*Frank to deadline-focused host Alex during New York: Linda Court*

the make

over method

Every makeover begins with a dream. Your dream room is no doubt an original, but chances are you're looking for one or more of seven essential things to make your room perfect. Turn the page to find out more about the seven decorating wishes. You're also about to discover ways to translate the ideas you find in this book into projects you can do at home. You'll learn to plan and shop like a pro and how to make smart trades on your time, money, and skills. So get going: You'll soon be creating fabulous rooms in 48 hours—the *Trading Spaces* way!

seven decorating wishes

Each episode of *Trading Spaces* begins with homeowners expressing their wishes and dreams for their rooms. That's where you'll start too. How many of the seven most common *Trading Spaces* wishes are you hoping for?

▲ Although you probably won't express your room makeover wishes on camera, as these homeowners had the opportunity to do, you will find that a concentrated brainstorming and planning session yields some creative redecorating ideas.

No matter how short you are on leisure time, daydreaming can be part of your strategic plan. Dreams can be shaped and reshaped while you do everyday activities—eat, drive, work, exercise, and, of course, sleep. Even a long, leisurely soak in the tub can be productive if you picture your dream room as you soak.

Every episode of *Trading Spaces* begins with homeowners detailing their dreams and wishes for their rooms; that's where you'll begin too. Picture the room you plan to transform and think of words and images you might use to describe your vision to your favorite *Trading Spaces* designer. How do you want the room to look, feel, and function? If you're like most homeowners, one or more of the following seven common decorating wishes will be on your list:

▲ADD MORE COLOR

▲ADD MORE COLOR The request for more color easily tops the wish list of most *Trading Spaces* homeowners. Color is one of the decorative elements you can achieve with only small investments in time—paint, pillows, area rugs, artwork, duvets, and slipcovers are some favorite quick-change options. In an especially large space (see Frank's big, dramatic red bedroom makeover on page 134), enlist the services of one or more friends to help paint. Or make a striking color statement with one "wow" feature; red walls with dark walnut glaze provide the "wow" in Christi's elegant study redo on page 62. Use slipcovers—ready-made or custom—to jump-start a new color scheme, or take a different do-it-yourself approach and wrap a bench or coffee tabletop with batting and fabric. To see the colorful results this can produce, check out Edward's Southwestern-style family room on page 126.

▼INCREASE COMFORT Without comfort, style doesn't matter. Understandably, people want to be comfortable in their own homes. Adding more pillows and sink-in seating is one option; however, sometimes getting comfortable involves rearranging existing furnishings. For example, Hildi helped a bachelor and his daughter live comfortably in a studio apartment by making one bed function as two sofas by day, a solution that anyone can re-create with stylish bed linens and pillows. To see Hildi's dramatic makeover, turn to page 30. The room arranging kit beginning on page 142 will give you further information on arranging furniture to achieve ultimate ease and comfort.

▶INCREASE COMFORT

▶CLEAR THE CLUTTER

◀CLEAR THE CLUTTER It's difficult to relax when a room is overwhelmed with belongings, even if they are all things you love. Editing out the excess is generally a job you can do in an afternoon; then you'll have the rest of the weekend to create a place for favorite things. For inspiration to tackle the job, see how Christi uses two sets of shelves and desks to organize the study featured on page 62. Hildi shows how a few fantastic pieces of artwork can be more effective than a full wall of art on page 110.

ACCENTUATE LIGHTING

▼**FRESHEN THE FLOOR** Because professionally installed new flooring can be expensive, many homeowners live with less-than-ideal floors for years. After you see some *Trading Spaces* ways to fix a floor fast, you may decide to take action on that old familiar floor of your own. Check out Hildi's striking wood parquet floor, for example, in the art-centered living room that begins on page 110. It's an elegant, understated surface that's suits many room styles and is doable in 48 hours.

▶FRESHEN THE FLOOR

▲**ACCENTUATE LIGHTING** If you're living in the dark, lighten up with a few well-placed lamps. And, of course, you need only an hour or so to swap the ceiling fan for a fan (or fixture) that better suits the room style, as Kia did in the bedroom on page 78. If you have a bit more time, personalize a lamp or shade by attaching embellishments with hot glue. Christi shows off one light-as-a-feather option on page 94.

STOW THE TELEVISION

◀**STOW THE TELEVISION** Whether you have a mammoth television set you want to hide—such as the one Laurie conceals in a closet on page 50—or you merely want to get audiovisual equipment off the floor—as was the case in Gen's botanical-style living room on page 118—stylish media storage does exist. If none of it suits your needs, create your own! For several instant storage solutions, check out the "Time Crunch" ideas for entertainment centers on page 49.

▶ DRESS THE WINDOWS

▲**DRESS THE WINDOWS** Deciding what you want to do with the windows in your room will be easier after you see the fast, stylish *Trading Spaces* window treatments throughout this book. No sewing skills are necessary for many looks—read up on the timesaving benefits of fusible webbing and hem tape on page 45. As you page along, keep your eyes open for quick and easy window treatments, including Edward's chic panels on page 57.

my wish list

Select a space in your own home that you want to make over and then run through the following list, checking off all the wishes you have for your room. As you tour the *Trading Spaces* "Makeovers in Motion" section that begins on page 28, use this checklist to note the page numbers where you find ideas you'd like to use.

☐ **ADD MORE COLOR**
My favorite color ideas are on pages
_____
_____
_____

☐ **INCREASE COMFORT**
My favorite comfort-creating ideas are on pages
_____
_____

☐ **CLEAR THE CLUTTER**
My favorite clutter-busting ideas are on pages
_____
_____
_____

☐ **ACCENTUATE LIGHTING**
My favorite lighting ideas are on pages
_____
_____
_____

☐ **STOW THE TELEVISION**
My favorite media storage ideas are on pages
_____
_____
_____

☐ **FRESHEN THE FLOOR**
My favorite flooring ideas are on pages
_____
_____

☐ **DRESS THE WINDOWS**
My favorite window treatment ideas are on pages
_____
_____

Whether you aim to satisfy one or more of the seven most common decorating wishes in your room, the results will add up to terrific style. Once you know what you're wishing for, looking at photographs can give you practical ideas of how to achieve your goal. Use this section to learn how to sleuth details from a photograph and translate what's pictured into projects you can do at home in a weekend or less.

Y ou may not have time to travel around to the various home shows or hours to spend at a designer's studio. However, evenings and weekends usually offer enough free time to browse through magazines and books in search of stylish rooms.

This book serves as an excellent starting point in your search for decorating inspiration:

• "Makeovers in Motion," for example, which begins on page 28, lets you tour 14 stylish spaces from the comfort of home.

• Each room tour begins with a "Get the Look" feature, a helpful breakdown of the elements used to create the character and style of the finished room.

• Each room tour recaps projects and personalities from the *Trading Spaces* episode, providing additional style inspiration.

• Photograph captions offer even more details, as well as tips for accomplishing similar projects more quickly.

Great headboard! —Innovative ideas, pp. 84, 134.

Nice linens. Maybe something more personal for me? —See p. 65.

Beautiful curtains, but can't sew. —See fusible webbing info, p. 45.

Very cool artwork.
Make my own?
—Instant artwork
ideas, p. 92.

Chic bedside table.
—Options on pp. 36,
94, 137.

Trading Spaces 48-Hour Makeovers identifies the special details in the featured rooms. After studying each room, you'll be able to do decorating detective work and analyze elements in any photograph of any beautiful room, such as the bedroom shown on pages 14 and 15 and the living room shown here. Here's how:

Identify. Study a favorite photograph and label the details you like best, such as the window treatments using adhesive-back notes.

Specify. Pinpoint the specific features you like and make a note of them, such as the fact that the window treatments are sheer.

Reference. With the help of this book, brainstorm ideas for achieving a similar look in fewer hours, such as looking for *Trading Spaces* rooms with sheer window treatments and writing the page number on the adhesive-back note. Features throughout this book, such as "Time Crunch," can help you tackle a variety of projects in less time.

Do I have room for display and storage? —Room arranging info, p. 142.

I want to get organized! —See p. 68.

Candles do make a difference. —More on p. 59.

Gorgeous wall color.
—Shop for painting
tools, p. 77.

Try this at next
cocktail party!
—Another tabletop
idea, p. 31.

Need a great
coffee table.
—More ideas,
p. 107.

Forget the stock market and get ready to learn about smart investment plans that will produce great results quickly. If you invest some effort in planning your decorating projects, they'll yield amazing benefits, including long-lasting style.

You've found the inspirational ideas, photos, and projects you want to use to transform your room. So where do you go from here?

▶ **TRADE COMMODITIES** You possess three commodities that you can choose to invest in your room makeover. These commodities are time, money, and skills. In the work triangle diagram, *right,* these commodities are shown as equal investments, illustrated by the three equal sides. However, you will probably make decisions that will lengthen or shorten one or more sides of the work triangle. Investing more on any one side of the triangle ultimately affects how much you need to invest in the other two sides of the triangle. Here are some examples:

SCENARIO #1: You have strong carpentry or sewing skills that you'll use on your decorating project. In this scenario, your biggest contribution to your decorating project will be your skills. Perhaps you're capable of constructing a custom bed frame efficiently or maybe you know how to sew your own slipcovers. Either way, you'll spend some time completing the project and probably save money by doing much of the work yourself.

SCENARIO #2: You have a wealth of cash to spend on your decorating project. In this scenario, your biggest contribution to the decorating project will be money. Strong financial backing gives you the option to hire someone to do the work; you'll save time, and your investment in skills can be limited.

SCENARIO #3: You have plenty of time available to invest in your decorating project. In this scenario, you'll save money by doing the work yourself. You'll also have enough time to learn the new skills that will allow you to complete the work without hiring professional help.

Time

Skills

Money

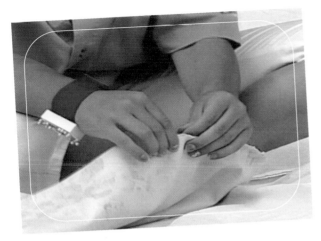

▶ **TAKE INVENTORY** Make a list of the skills, time, and money resources you have available. For example, do you have any of the following skills: carpentry, sewing, painting, design, electrical, or plumbing? Do you have a handy uncle or a friend with excellent decorating taste? If so, add their names to the "skills" portion of your inventory list. Check to see if any skills essential to your project are missing. Then determine whether you want to spend time learning the new skill (you may have to spend money on a class or seminar) or whether you'd rather spend money to hire someone to do the work for you.

When noting the time you have available, take into account weekends, evenings, and vacation time. Estimate how many hours you can spare each week. You may choose to invest only a few of these hours or all of them. Either way, it's smart to determine ahead of time what's reasonable.

Also write down the financial resources you want to contribute to accomplish the project. You may decide to use savings, borrow funds, or pay as you go. Consider trading skills with friends to save money (see page 20).

buying time

Wouldn't it be great if you could walk into a specialty store and say, "Um, I'm looking for some extra time." "Oh yes," the helpful employee replies, "we have plenty in Aisle 6!"

Although the scenario is far-fetched, you have nevertheless found what you're looking for. This book is rich in tips, tricks, and insider secrets—all designed to help you buy time and make the most of the hours you have available for decorating. Watch for the following recurring features:

▶ **THE DECORATING PANTRY** Use these information-packed sidebars to learn about the supplies you need to keep on hand to help you accomplish a wide range of decorating projects stylishly and quickly. Instead of rushing out and buying all these things today, make a list of the items and keep it handy in your wallet. Whenever you shop, check your list against weekly specials, bargain bins, and clearance racks to see whether any of the items are on sale. Then you can stock up. To store your decorating supplies, a shelf or two in a cabinet or closet and a few clear-plastic bins or shoeboxes will do nicely. You could also employ a large drawer and some wire dividers to organize your decorating pantry.

▶ **TIME CRUNCH** These sidebars offer dozens of time-conscious decorating ideas. You'll find helpful tips on buying double-duty furnishings, creating media equipment storage, building home office desks, and adorning ceilings, furniture, walls, doors, floors, windows, and accessories.

▶ **FAST PROJECT INSPIRED BY THE SHOW** These two-page sections offer more stylish ways to decorate in record time. Lists of materials and tools accompany clear step-by-step instructions, making each project quick and easy. You'll love these superfast ideas for making nightstands and a home office desk, dressing windows, arranging beautiful shelves and mantels, organizing chaotic bookcases, creating dynamic tabletops for entertaining, painting focal point walls, fashioning headboards, and making your own artwork, lighting, outdoor containers, and cabinet hardware.

▶**WORK ON PAPER** As you consider the projects you want to do to complete your room makeover, keep the work triangle in mind. For example, if your painting skills are good and your carpentry skills are lacking, you may decide to paint the walls yourself and hire a carpenter to reface the fireplace. Make these decisions and write them down. The more planning you do beforehand, the more time you will ultimately save while you work on your room makeover.

▶**START A MAKEOVER FILE** Use a three-ring binder or scrapbook to corral all your ideas, photos, project information, and checklists. Here are a few of the things you can include in your file:

  - ▶ Inspirational photographs
  - ▶ Project how-to information
  - ▶ Fabric swatches, paint colors, or other material samples
  - ▶ Master list of projects
  - ▶ List of your skills and the skills of others who are readily available to you
  - ▶ Business cards of electricians, carpenters, plumbers, sewing professionals, or painters
  - ▶ A list of materials and tools needed to complete each project. Use the "Checklist for Success" on page 26 to determine whether you have everything you need.
  - ▶ Detailed floor plan of the space. This will help you

avoid buying or building furnishings that won't fit. The "Room Arranging Kit" that begins on page 142 explains how to make a floor plan and furniture templates.

  - ▶ List of important measurements. Measure all window dimensions and furniture sizes. Take these measurements with you when you shop to help you select appropriately sized accessories and coverings.
  - ▶ Master schedule. Use "Schedule the Makeover," *opposite,* as a guide to create a rough schedule of your own weekend makeover. "Follow *Trading Spaces,*" on page 24, provides another visual guide for establishing a schedule.

▶**TRADE SKILLS** It's OK to work alone; however, you'll get work done more quickly if you enlist the help of family and friends. Children as young as 7 or 8 can stuff pillows; older children can sand furniture and paint walls, for example. Teenagers can help paint furniture or assist in carpentry projects.

If you invite friends over to help with the makeover, make a party of it. Have snacks and beverages on hand and put on some lively music. Make plans to help your friends with their next project. Another option: If you lack experience in one skill, find a friend who has the skill and then trade. For example, if you are a good carpenter yet lack electrical skills, find a friend who has electrical skills. Ask your friend to replace your ceiling fan with a more attractive fixture, then use your carpentry skills to build something, such as a bench, for your friend.

Add to your Makeover File a list of the tools you think you'll need to do the projects efficiently. Check your workshop inventory and buy what you need ahead of time. Use the "Shop Smart" tips on page 22.

▶**PAY A PRO** If you build lopsided shelves and have to redo them, you're ultimately spending more money and more time than it would have taken to hire a professional. In some cases, you're better off paying someone skilled; that person will save you time and labor. Ask friends, neighbors, and coworkers for recommendations. Home centers and specialty stores also may be able to recommend someone. For example, ask fabric store employees who does their sewing; ask the tile dealer to recommend a skilled tile installer.

▶**UPGRADE TOOLS** Having the proper tools will make your projects faster and easier. When painting, for example, purchase quality paint and supplies; the right tools, such as a roller with an extendable handle, can save time. If you plan to build shelves, a quality circular saw saves labor and yields better results than a handsaw.

schedule the makeover

Here's a sample schedule for accomplishing a room makeover in a weekend. The schedule assumes that you have at least one helper and that you plan ahead and purchase all needed supplies, materials, and tools beforehand.

▶DAY 1

MORNING:
- Eat a good breakfast
- Clear the room
- Tape off woodwork
- Position drop cloths
- Fill holes in walls
- Paint ceiling

Lunch Break

AFTERNOON:
- Apply paint to walls
- Measure and map out pieces that need to be cut for larger woodworking projects, such as shelves or a bench
- Cut the pieces and assemble large woodworking projects

Dinner Break

EVENING:
- Sand and prime any existing furniture you plan to paint; stain or prime newly built pieces
- Do prep work for tomorrow's projects
- Get a good night's sleep

▶DAY 2

MORNING:
- Eat a good breakfast
- Top coat primed furniture; polyurethane stained pieces
- Cut fabric for pillows, window treatments, and slipcovers

Lunch Break

AFTERNOON:
- Sew pillows, window treatments, and slipcovers
- Stuff pillows and stitch closed
- Embellish lighting and/or bedding
- Do fast artwork projects

Dinner Break

EVENING:
- Remove debris from room
- Position furniture
- Hang artwork
- Hang window treatments
- Hang stationary lighting

shop smart

◀ Christi considers a bolt of fabric. If you have questions about sewing or choosing the best fabric for your project, fabric store employees can usually offer good advice.

▶ Laurie ponders some dishware patterns. When you're hunting for dishware and other decorative items, keep in mind that large discount stores generally stock a good selection.

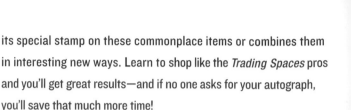

The *Trading Spaces* crew typically rolls into town only one day prior to the filming of an episode. Designers, carpenters, and crew have only 24 hours to completely prepare for 48 hours of redecorating—under the constant scrutiny of video cameras and with fans stopping them during their shopping for autographs and pictures. It's an added challenge that the designers are frequently visiting the cities for the first time; before they can get the right supplies, they have to find a national retail store quickly. Some of the rooms featured on the show contain one-of-a-kind items/materials (an antique chest of drawers, gorgeous fabric from a salvage dealer, or a piece of beloved art, for example). However, much of the stuff you see in the rooms comes from national retailers. The *Trading Spaces* crew puts

◀ Amy Wynn and Doug stroll the aisles of a home center. Shop these venues when you want to save time by gathering lots of supplies in one stop.

its special stamp on these commonplace items or combines them in interesting new ways. Learn to shop like the *Trading Spaces* pros and you'll get great results—and if no one asks for your autograph, you'll save that much more time!

▶ **WHY?** When you shop smart, you save time. Smart shopping lets you spend less time in stores and more time working. And you'll work more efficiently when everything you need for a project is on hand.

▶ **WHEN?** Post your shopping list on the refrigerator for a day or two to give yourself time to think about additional materials or tools you might need.

Shop home centers and fabric, crafts, and hardware stores during the week to avoid the weekend crowds. Weekday midmornings and early afternoons are typically the quietest times to get your shopping done.

Call local home centers or hardware stores and ask store personnel what hours their store is least busy. If you know you have an unusual item on your list, call around first to find out which store has the item in stock.

▶ **WHERE?** Large home centers offer one-stop shopping so you don't waste time driving from one store to the next.

Discount stores can supply most of the rest of your decorating needs, including fabric, pillows, bed linens, bath towels, shower curtains, rugs, small furnishings, glassware, houseplants and containers, and other decorative accessories.

Save time at the store by grouping like items on your list, such as bath items, lighting needs, and houseplants. You'll avoid unnecessary wandering back and forth between departments.

Limit the number of specialty stores you shop. Although a florist may offer beautiful flower arrangements, most discount stores or crafts stores carry a variety of floral accessories and arrangements. In addition, discount and crafts stores will most likely have other items you need to purchase for your projects.

Shop online for hard-to-find items or for any item that you would have to drive a great distance to obtain. Also, if regular business hours aren't convenient for you, you can shop online far into the night. Allow plenty of time for shipping and for reordering, if necessary.

▶**WHAT?** Have a list in hand when you leave the house; otherwise you'll probably forget something and need to make a second trip.

Read the packaging or directions for each specialty item you purchase (window treatments, ready-to-assemble furniture, lighting, and so on). Verify that you have all the supplies, materials, and tools needed to install the specialty item.

Take a moment to study the photograph on the packaging too. Manufacturers can offer some great decorating ideas and also point out what's practical. For example, looking at a photograph on a comforter set may remind you that you need two new bed pillows to accompany the shams in the package.

Save time by having the home center cut sheet goods or moldings to the sizes you need.

▲ Amy Wynn and Christi gather supplies at the home center. Cut shopping time in half in large stores by taking someone with you and splitting up the list.

When shopping for fabric, purchase material that won't fray when you cut it; that way, you won't have to hem. Blanket fleece, velvet, felt, leather, and faux leather are a few no-fray options.

Use the "Checklist for Success" on page 26 to see if you have everything you need to complete your projects.

▶**WHO?** Take a helper to the store with you and split up the list. If you need to shop two stores, send your helper to one.

If checkout lines are long, have your helper proceed to the checkout line while you wrap up final selection details.

Ask store staff to move, carry, and load heavy or large-scale items. Most retail salespeople have access to dollies, hand trucks, and other tools that make transporting large, heavy purchases easier.

▶**HOW?** Check that your vehicle has enough space to transport whatever you are buying; otherwise, build time into your schedule for multiple trips. Or put money in your budget to pay for delivery service.

Another option is to plan to borrow or rent a pickup truck if you don't own one.

◀ Doug checks a list of supplies. Reduce shopping time by taking along a list of the things you need. Group like items on the list to avoid backtracking through the aisles.

▶ Gen pauses at the paint chips. Save time selecting paint by asking your paint dealer for a full deck of paint chip cards that you can keep on hand at home.

follow
trading
spaces

Tag along—from start to finish—and see how to transform a room in only a weekend, the *Trading Spaces* way!

LO1:02:09.15

start

▸ **MOVE OUT** Start Day 1 by clearing out the room. Doing so gives you plenty of room to work and protects your furniture from accidental paint splatters.

▸ **PLAN IT** Plan what you'd like to change about the look of your room. (Shop for necessary supplies too.)

LO1:31:08.14

▸ **WALL FLAIR** Start Day 2 by applying or installing any decorative wall treatments.

LO1:32:42.20

▸ **SEW AND GO** Cut, hem, create, and alter any window treatments, pillows, bedding, and table linens for the room.

▸ **FRAME UP** Create easy custom art for the space.

▶ **PAINT TIME** Bring attitude to your walls and ceilings with a base coat of your chosen paint color.

▶ **CUT AND BUILD** While the base coat dries, begin work on any major carpentry projects.

▶ **SOFT STUFF** Move on to major fabric projects, such as reupholstering furniture.

▶ **WOOD WONDERS** After applying a second coat of paint to the walls and ceiling (if needed), apply primer and paint or stain to any new furniture you've built.

▶ **BRIGHT DELIGHT** Install any new light fixtures in the nearly finished room.

finish

▶ **LAST CHANCE** After moving the furniture back into the room, add draperies, pillows, lamps, artwork, and other decorative items.

You're inspired and you have a plan; you know how to shop and how to work the plan. Use these two pages to double-check that you have everything you need, then set your 48-hour timer—you're ready to redo your room in a weekend.

▶ PAINTING WALLS AND CEILINGS

- ☐ Clean walls
- ☐ ___ yards of painter's masking tape
- ☐ Drop cloths
- ☐ Spackling compound
- ☐ Putty knife
- ☐ Fine-grit sandpaper
- ☐ ___ gallons of primer
- ☐ ___ gallons of paint
- ☐ Paint can opener and stir sticks
- ☐ Rags to clean up drips and spills
- ☐ Assorted paintbrushes
- ☐ Rollers, extension poles, and paint trays
- ☐ Fans (to aid in drying paint)
- ☐ Step stools (or stepladders for rooms with high ceilings)
- ☐ Several movable lamps/lights to gauge paint coverage

▶ INSPIRATION AND PLANNING

- ☐ I have an image in mind (or pictures from printed publications) of what the finished room will look like.
- ☐ I have images in mind (or pictures from printed publications) of each finished project.
- ☐ I have paint and fabric samples.
- ☐ I have all critical measurements handy, including:
  - ☐ Room dimensions
  - ☐ Window and door dimensions
  - ☐ Key furnishing dimensions
- ☐ I have a Makeover File assembled to help me stay organized.

▶ SAFETY EQUIPMENT

- ☐ Gloves
- ☐ Dust masks
- ☐ Goggles
- ☐ Work boots
- ☐ Earplugs
- ☐ Painter caps or bandannas
- ☐ First aid kit or easy access to a well-stocked medicine cabinet

▶ HELPERS

- ☐ I've asked people to help.
- ☐ They have the skills to do the projects.
- ☐ I've hired skilled labor for some steps/tasks, if needed.
- ☐ All helpers know when to arrive and whether they're responsible for bringing anything.
- ☐ I have a variety of music on hand to keep my helpers energized.

- ☐ I have supplies collected to feed and care for my helpers, including:
  - ☐ Paper plates and cups
  - ☐ Beverages
  - ☐ Snacks (both salty and sweet!)
  - ☐ Basic sandwich/salad fixings
  - ☐ Take-out menus
  - ☐ Money to pay for deliveries

▶ PAINTING FURNITURE OR CABINETS

- [ ] Wood filler
- [ ] Assorted sandpaper
- [ ] Steel wool, in various densities
- [ ] Straightedge and measuring tape
- [ ] Tack cloths
- [ ] Painter's masking tape
- [ ] Primer
- [ ] Paint
- [ ] Rags
- [ ] Disposable mixing buckets and containers
- [ ] Drop cloths
- [ ] Assorted paintbrushes and artist's brushes
- [ ] Specialty painting tools (stamps, stencils, combing tool, etc.)
- [ ] Specialty paint (glazes, texturing agents, etc.)
- [ ] Clear polyurethane sealer
- [ ] New drawer pulls, knobs, handles, and hinges

▶ CLEANUP

- [ ] Brooms and dustpans
- [ ] Garbage bags
- [ ] Dust rags and paper towels
- [ ] All-purpose cleaners
- [ ] Mops
- [ ] Buckets
- [ ] Vacuum cleaner and attachments

▶ CARPENTRY PROJECTS

- [ ] Measuring tape
- [ ] Carpenter's level
- [ ] Straightedge
- [ ] Chalk line
- [ ] Pencil
- [ ] Stud finder
- [ ] Drill
- [ ] Assorted drill bits
- [ ] Assorted screwdrivers
- [ ] Hammer
- [ ] Nail set
- [ ] Pliers
- [ ] Assorted wrenches
- [ ] Tool belt
- [ ] Handsaw
- [ ] Circular saw
- [ ] Jigsaw
- [ ] Sawhorses
- [ ] Clamps
- [ ] Fasteners (screws, finishing nails)
- [ ] Woodworker's glue

▶ FABRIC PROJECTS

- [ ] Sharp, quality scissors
- [ ] Assorted thread, needles, and pins
- [ ] Marking pen or pencil
- [ ] Sewing machine
- [ ] Fusible hem tape
- [ ] Iron and ironing board
- [ ] Cloth measuring tape
- [ ] Hook-and-loop tape
- [ ] ___ yards of fabric
- [ ] Loose acrylic batting (for stuffing pillows)
- [ ] Clip-on curtain rings
- [ ] Covered-button kits
- [ ] Specialty buttons, trims, edging, etc.
- [ ] Staple gun and staples
- [ ] Fabric glue

▶ EMBELLISHMENT PROJECTS

- [ ] Hot-glue gun
- [ ] Glue gun sticks (melt-point appropriate for the project)
- [ ] Fusible hem tape and webbing
- [ ] Assorted thread and needles
- [ ] Scissors
- [ ] Straightedge
- [ ] Assorted buttons
- [ ] Assorted ribbon
- [ ] Assorted cording
- [ ] Assorted fringe and tassels
- [ ] Grommets and grommet tool
- [ ] Specialty paints (for fabric, metals, ceramics, etc.)
- [ ] Assorted artist's brushes
- [ ] Metallic leafing kit
- [ ] Decoupage medium
- [ ] Decoupage images (printed on one-sided, heavy paper stock)

If you've ever wished you could freeze-frame your favorite *Trading Spaces* rooms so you could study the details longer, this is the opportunity you've been looking for. Take all the time you need to tour the stylish spaces that follow; dissect and digest the details as you relive the episodes. Then read on to learn more inside secrets that will help you accomplish your own room makeovers and creative projects. Best of all, you'll find out how to make a dream room happen in only 48 hours.

s motion

multipurpose Parisian

Designers are often asked to make one room work like two. Hildi went a step further when she signed up to redo this studio apartment: She used a sharp pencil to fit a houseful of function into one modest space. Touches of Paris prove that even small spaces have room for elegance.

Mild temperatures

Soft mango walls cloak the once all-white room with inviting warmth. Chocolate brown paint on the ceiling (and even on the carpeting!) creates intimacy—a worthy goal in even the smallest of spaces.

Fabric layers

Draperies make any window grander. This panel extends over an entire wall adding soft texture and subtle interest.

Small interests

Most artwork in the room is simple and smaller scale. Large white mats and matching frames create continuity and a pleasing contemporary look in a jiffy.

Illuminating idea

Built-in lighting prevents the arch around the platform sofa bed from becoming a foreboding shadowy spot. The fixtures also help spotlight the artwork.

Attention, please

Even the smallest room needs a fabulous focal point. Behind the sofa bed, the dramatic oversize photograph is one that Hildi snapped in Paris. Turn the page to learn the clever secret behind this piece

Finishing flourish

Every room looks better with touches of black for style and hints of metal for eye-pleasing shine. A pair of silvery bowls on the table features fruit and greenery for added color.

Straight talk

Clean-lined designs, such as this custom-made platform sofa bed, prevent the room from feeling overcrowded. This built-in divides the studio into two spaces.

Not busy

Solid mango fabrics introduce sophistication and don't overwhelm the small space like too much pattern might.

This efficiency apartment was the right size for the bachelor tenant most of the time; however, he didn't feel comfortable inviting anyone over because a pair of twin beds—and not much else—dominated the all-white space. In addition, the room didn't comfortably accommodate his young daughter's weekend visits.

Hildi sets a high goal of making the space superfunctional and ultrastylish: "We have to figure out how to fit in an office area, a social area, a dining area, a sleeping area for him, a little special

▲ Paint serves as a superfast refresher for almost any surface. In this apartment, the walls, ceiling, and furniture all got new looks with paint; this pair of thrift store bench bases was quickly primed and spray-painted brown. The painting didn't stop there: Noting that the worn carpeting was glued down and might require untold hours of labor to remove, Hildi opted to paint it instead! She used a roller equipped with an extension pole to apply latex paint thinned with a special conditioner. Before painting carpet, check with your local paint dealer to discuss additives that might allow the fibers to remain flexible after painting. Or investigate the availability of carpet dyes in your area.

▶**before**

▶Orlando: Smith Street

This efficiency apartment, occupied by a single father, lacks order and style. The space needs to work better for daily living, and the tenant needs space for entertaining and dining. Because the tenant's daughter stays some weekends, Hildi wants to create a private space that the little girl can call her own.

sleeping and play area for his daughter, and a theater area," Hildi says.

The key to the makeover is a built-in platform topped with an arch, custom-made by Amy Wynn; the platform holds the pair of twin beds side by side. During the day, bolsters and pillows allow the beds to serve as sofas. A large screen—displaying an oversize photograph of a Paris street scene—pulls down for privacy and divides the apartment into two sleeping areas. When only one sleeping area is needed, the screen rolls up so the two twin beds can function as one king-size bed.

▶ superfunctional furniture

Save time and space by purchasing furniture that can quickly transform to serve more than one purpose.

▶ **OTTOMANS** occupy only a few square feet and can perform a variety of functions. Place a pair beneath a window as an impromptu window seat. Locate one beside a chair and top the cushion with a tray to hold beverages and books. Position an ottoman in front of a chair or sofa to prop up feet. When company arrives, slide the ottomans wherever you need extra seating.

▶ **DAYBEDS** and foldout sofa beds allow a room to function as a living space or office during the day and convert to a guest room as needed. To sleep more than one person without sacrificing floor space, include a trundle bed in the guest room.

▶ **ARMOIRES** make ideal storage units for audiovisual equipment. If you purchase a model that features foldaway desk space, you'll have a handy office. Also consider equipping an armoire or tall cabinet as a sewing center, a crafts or hobby station, a potting compartment, or an ultraorganized gift-wrapping area.

▶ **BENCHES** with storage beneath a lift-up lid or equipped with pullout drawers below the seat can be used to form compact banquette seating around a breakfast table. Or use benches to offer storage and seating beneath a window or in a small niche in the bathroom.

▶ **CONSOLE TABLES** typically require only a sliver of space and offer a surface for display or serving buffet-style dinners. Add a fabric skirt and a shelf or two below the tabletop for storing linens and dishware, books, or even a television and stereo.

◀ To make a dividing screen in record time, have a photograph or other artwork transferred to canvas. To hang this divider screen, Hildi purchased a standard roller shade in the desired width and removed the plain shade. She then used a staple gun to secure the Parisian-scene roller shade to the remaining rod, which features a roller mechanism that raises and lowers the screen when needed.

On the living room side of the space, a pair of slipcovered thrift store chairs teams up with two benches, the sofa bed, and a table to allow flexibility for dining and social gatherings. A newly painted cabinet houses the television and stereo.

To make more space in the main room, Hildi eliminated the tenant's desk and repositioned existing wire components in a closet so that one shelf hangs at desktop height. With the closet door open, the tenant can pull up a chair and use the shelf, topped with glass or wood, as a writing surface. This setup suffices for a home office.

Though the makeover went about $36 over budget, Hildi playfully points out that she actually created more than one room.

The tenant is delighted with the results. "This is nothing that I imagined," he says, "and better than what I could have imagined."

▶ A bounty of underutilized storage space may already exist in your house. Look beneath beds and staircases, for example, to discover several cubic feet of storage space. Add slide-out storage compartments for convenience. On the daughter's side of the platform, the area beneath the bed is left open for storing toys and other belongings. (On the living room side, the area beneath the sofa bed is enclosed for an uncluttered look.) The screen is down to create a private spot for the young girl.

beads

Decorative beads add a custom touch to all sorts of ready-made items, from drapery tiebacks and curtain panels to throw pillows and table linens. Keep an assortment of these affordably priced gems on hand in your decorating pantry:

▸ **SEED BEADS** Seed beads are small round beads that range in size from 2 to 2.5 millimeters. They come in nearly every color and are ideal for decorating lampshades, picture frames, and pottery. Seed beads can be strung on fishing line, or attached to almost any smooth surface with clear-drying glue or decoupage medium.

▸ **CHARMS** Extremely popular with the beading crowd, charms can be strung like beads or tacked on with thread to customize all kinds of surfaces and objects. Because charms are pricey, pick only the ones that are perfect for a project.

▸ **GLASS BEADS** These multifaceted beads range in size from 4 to 10 millimeters and look great when sewn onto a favorite fabric or hung from a shade pull. While handmade glass beads are expensive, affordable mass-produced ones are available in bulk. String 8 or 10 of them on a large wire hoop earring and add a single decorative charm to make a beautiful wine charm. (Wine charms loop around the stem of a wineglass to help guests keep track of their drinks.)

▸ **PRESTRUNG BEADS** Save yourself some time and let someone else do the tedious work of stringing beads. Prestrung beads and beaded ribbons and trim can be attached instantly with a little hot glue; they provide a great way to speed up the decorating process.

▲ When the daughter is away, the screen can roll up in the evening to let the twin beds function as one king-size sleeping area. (One king-size fitted sheet can slip over the twin mattresses.)

▶ ceiling dress-ups

Designers often refer to the ceiling as the fifth wall; to enhance its status, consider using one of these fast fix-ups.

▶ **FABRIC** Staple fabric to the ceiling to introduce fast color overhead. Avoid tedious ironing before installation by choosing fabric that looks great wrinkled, such as gauze, and install the lengths in billowy waves.

▶ **SEA GRASS** Mats made of sea grass are inexpensive and can be found online and at import stores. Use a staple gun to secure the mat to the ceiling, covering the entire expanse. Or create an inset look by outlining the mat with moldings secured to the ceiling with construction adhesive.

▶ **STAMPS** Designs created with stamps aren't only for walls, and they're faster than stencils. Consider flowers or animals in a child's room, fruit or veggies in the kitchen, and geometric shapes for the family room.

◀ Purchasing a precut wooden round (available at some home centers in a variety of sizes), building a base, and painting the entire piece brown produces a stylish table in only a few hours. Hildi sized this one to quickly transition from entertaining to dining duty.

Urn Undercover

Visit a local garden center or peruse your favorite garden catalogs and online sources to find an urn that suits the height of your bed.

Look for a heavy urn, one that won't easily topple, and choose one that isn't too large in diameter for a glass top. Top the urn with two glass tabletop rounds, stacked one on top of the other. Apply adhesive-back vinyl dots, if needed, to stabilize the bottom glass layer.

Between the glass layers, slip in decorative paper items to conceal the urn interior. Vintage seed packets are shown here; you could also use old photographs, postcards, pressed flowers, or fabric—anything flat.

● ● ● ● ● ● ● ● ● ● ● ● ● ● ●
In a few minutes

right-now nightstands

Everyone needs a landing spot beside the bed for an alarm clock, a few books, a glass of water, and a reading lamp. While you could go out and buy an ordinary bedside table, why not put together one with more character? These two nightstands require almost no time at all—shop and prop, and they're ready to use and admire.

Stool Style

A vintage stool still dressed in peeling paint—here, a pleasing shade of Depression-era green—makes a charming side table. Set the stool beside the bed—on a rug, if you wish—and use the seat as the tabletop.

To find a metal or wood kitchen stool, keep your eyes open at garage sales, flea markets, or even in your grandmother's attic. This stool was discovered in use behind the counter at a garden center and was purchased for $15.

In a few minutes

Low-cost lighting
Clustered paper lanterns serve as a fun and funky ceiling fixture; a small-scale pair of sconces flanks the window.

Cool thinking
The black and white painted stripe brings graphic interest to the room and won't go out of style.

Sporty fabric
Black tape and orange jersey fabric serve as hockey-theme tiebacks for the dividing draperies—with little time investment.

Panel discussion
Floor-to-ceiling drapery panels between the sleeping and activity areas can be closed when the 9-year-old wants a break from his younger brothers.

Stage right
What kid doesn't love a stage? When the boy is older, this sleeping platform will still have its appeal. Black carpeting covers the plywood-and-2×4 structure, adding comfort and enhancing the awesome look.

DESIGNED BY GENEVIEVE

boys' retreat

It's important to design children's rooms for their rapidly changing interests. This bedroom, which Gen designed for a 9-year-old boy who loves sports, meets the challenge. Two younger brothers hang out here too, so Gen's clever tactics provide room for privacy and group activities.

►before

►Pennsylvania: Tremont Dr.

This boy's bedroom features some interesting architectural bonuses and generous square footage. However, white walls and bare windows make the space feel empty and dull. Gen's challenge is to create a space that the boy thinks is cool and to build in some elements that can easily grow with his changing tastes.

Childhood can be full of great memories, and an awesome bedroom like this one could be one of them. A 9-year-old boy who loves hockey and other sports is the lucky recipient of this design by Gen. His parents asked for a "cool" bedroom and also wanted the space to continue as a gathering place for the boy and his younger brothers.

Gen says the room will be "fun, playful, whimsical but cool, because he's going to be graduating into the teens. He's very sporty, but we have to celebrate his other sides, like art."

◀ Gen says that rather than paint huge sports logos in the room, she wanted to get a sporty look "in a more sophisticated fashion with photography." She went to a sports collectibles store and found autographed pictures of pro hockey players. Though Gen admits the photos were pricey, they were a fast way to bring framed artwork into the room, and the boy is sure to love them.

> **Our country is quickly becoming something other than what we pride ourselves upon. If one was to judge us by our interiors alone, we would be a nation called Beigeland. A generic, oatmeal sort of people without a lot of passion, diversity, or spirit. It's really sad.**
>
> **We are not a beige people! We're the most diverse nation on the planet, and where we live should reflect our personalities, our life experiences, and our joys. Trash the hesitation surrounding the fear of the unknown and bring color into your lives. Ask yourself what colors give you joy. Look at your favorite foods, sweaters, and vacation destinations and grab that palette. Paint! Get rid of all your overhead lighting, trash the fluorescents, and grab some dimmers and lamps. You can do this all for under $100; all you need is the drive.**
>
> **—Genevieve Gorder**

Elevating one side of the room with a platform visually defines the space as two distinct areas—one for sleeping and studying and one for hanging out with brothers and friends. Black carpeting covers the platform, which was constructed of 2×4s and plywood; the carpeting is a neutral element that's pleasing for the younger set (the jet black color is cool) as well as comfortable.

A pair of built-in desks flanks the platform, offering space for reading, art projects, and homework.

Floor-to-ceiling curtain panels gather at the foot of the sleep/study area and can be closed to provide privacy from the other half of the room. That half is furnished with shelves and low chairs; it's a place to hang out, watch TV, and play video games.

◀ Kids can be messy; plastic chairs clean up quickly. Set low to the floor, the chairs are ideal for the younger set; they're also low-cost, so they're a great way to add accent colors that the boy might want to change in the future.

▶ Custom lighting can be relatively easy to create. In this boy's bedroom, a piece of lattice provides a stylish grid for suspending a group of low-cost paper lanterns. The lattice also conceals the lamp cords.

Though the theme of the room is sports, Gen provides for future changes by painting the walls and ceiling leaf green, a color that functions here as a neutral. Partway up the walls a bold black and white stripe races around the room and serves as a reference to the boy's favorite professional hockey team, the Philadelphia Flyers. Gen points out that the stripe design is flexible; it "could just look like a hip lounge when you are 15," she says. For now, orange and black accents play up the hockey team colors. In the future the accent colors could easily change and still work with the green walls and the black and white stripe.

Lattice on the ceiling and a collection of green and white paper lanterns finish the room with a playful flourish.

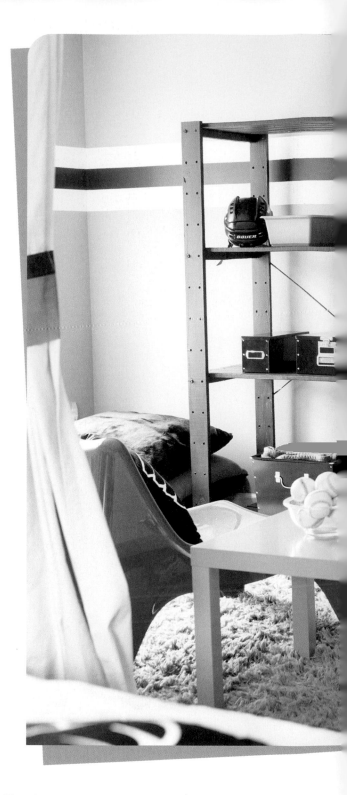

◀ Painted stripes are a simple project, whether you want them to run vertically or horizontally. Use a level and a pencil to mark straight lines; keep edges crisp by outlining stripes with painter's tape before painting. Use your thumbnail to burnish the edge of the tape so that paint doesn't bleed underneath. Rather than paint the window treatment with a matching stripe, Gen saved time by using black tape.

◄Shelves like these can be purchased unfinished and ready-to-assemble from discount stores. Paint or stain assembled shelving units to suit the decor. Black paint brings this unit in line with the new look of the room. The shelving unit acts as an entertainment center and provides display space.

From the Designers

►GENEVIEVE GORDER

Q If *Trading Spaces* offered you a choice of more time or more money on a particular episode, which would you choose?

A More time. I think the best part about the show is that it not only challenges the designers to be art students again—thinking creatively and resourcefully—it also gives the viewer projects that almost anyone can realistically afford (including kids).

Often when a lot of money is involved, a designer can become less of an artist and more of a glamorized shopper in my eyes. More time would allow me to create more and with more attention.

Q What three items do you recommend homeowners keep on hand in their decorating pantries?

A "Decorating pantry?" Ha ha ha! Well, if you are rare enough to have a decorating pantry, I would suggest you not keep just three things but keep all the things you collect for no apparent reason. There is a reason you are hanging on to these items. Whether they be a collection of tin plates from some garage sale or a group of old football helmets, there is a sort of sentimental attraction going on. Keep these items as inspirational storage. They may not become the focal point of a room but may just inspire a color palette or offshoot idea.

If you don't have a pantry, which I myself don't, an 11×14-inch hardcover black sketchbook (as well as an art closet) works great for collecting ideas and keeps everything much more organized. People will always want to know what you have in there.

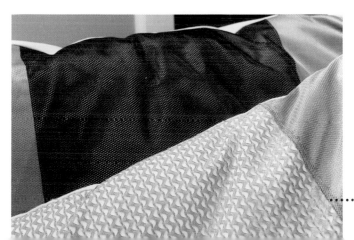

◄Even the pillows get in on the sports theme. These pillows are covered in fabric used to make sports jerseys.

fast project
inspired by the show

no-sew panels and pillows

In an afternoon

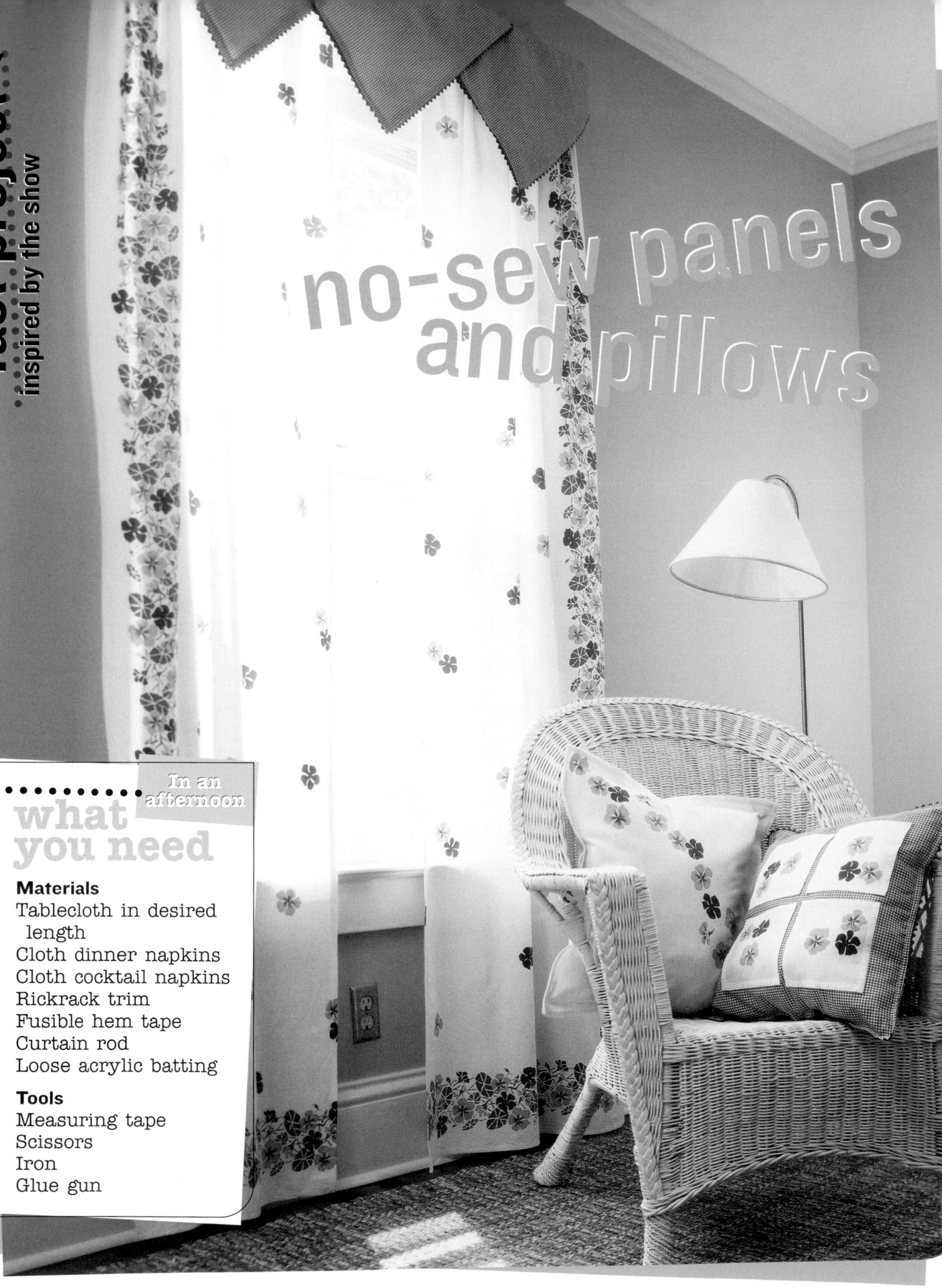

what you need

Materials
Tablecloth in desired length
Cloth dinner napkins
Cloth cocktail napkins
Rickrack trim
Fusible hem tape
Curtain rod
Loose acrylic batting

Tools
Measuring tape
Scissors
Iron
Glue gun

Your windows and chairs don't have to stay bare just because you don't sew. If you own an iron, custom curtain panels, valances, and accent pillows can be yours—all in an afternoon. Here's how.

This window treatment and the coordinating accent pillows began as a 102-inch-long tablecloth and complementary dinner and cocktail napkins, *right.* Though the pattern is vintage, the tablecloth is new. Reproduction patterns are widely available, so you won't have to cut up anything valuable. You may prefer a more contemporary pattern or solid colors.

1. To make the curtain panels, cut the tablecloth in half lengthwise. Following the package directions, use fusible hem tape to finish the cut edge of each panel. Fold over the top few inches of each panel and secure with fusible hem tape, leaving enough room for a rod pocket. Slip the panels onto a rod and hang.

2. To form the valance, select complementary dinner napkins. Hot-glue rickrack around the edges of each napkin. Drape the napkins over the top of the rod to form a valance.

3. To make accent pillows, take two dinner napkins and join them along three sides with fusible hem tape. Iron four complementary cocktail napkins onto one side of the pillow. Fill the pillow with loose acrylic batting. Secure the open end with fusible hem tape.

the decorating pantry

fusible webbing

This paper-backed man-made netting melts when heated by an iron, creating a sturdy bond between layers of fabric, felt, or heat-resistant paper. Make rod pockets, hem curtain panels, create wall hangings, or attach appliquéd designs to any heat-resistant material without ever touching a needle and thread.

The material is available in both sheet and tape form (you may have heard the tape referred to as hem tape); it also comes in a variety of strengths that let you adhere fabrics as delicate as silk or as sturdy as denim or velvet. Read package directions carefully to see if the product you are considering is suitable for your intended use. Fusible webbing is available at crafts and fabric stores.

Here are a few other simple *Trading Spaces*-inspired projects that use fusible webbing:

▶ **MAKE A SPRING OR FALL TABLE RUNNER** using two equal lengths of burlap in two colors. Cut one a few inches wider than the other; stack the narrower piece on top of the wider piece. Add colorful fabric leaves or flowers. Adhere all the materials with iron-on fusible webbing.

▶ **COVER EXISTING CHAIR PADS** or create slipcovers to match your table runner; use complementary-color fabrics and join the pieces with additional webbing.

45

Molded image
A popcorn-texture ceiling made it difficult to achieve a crisp edge for a painted color inset. Narrow molding covers the feathered edges of the paint and provides a crisp, clean border.

Minimal shelves
Plain, straight-lined shelves let the artwork take the spotlight.

Gentle background
Soft yellow makes a windowless corner cheery and sets the stage for pleasant dining.

Understated elegance
Black and white family photos become chic artwork when unified with wide white mats and thin black frames.

Goodbye, brass
An outdated brass-tube dining table receives a stylish—and quick— update with chrome spray paint. Soft, buttery yellow fabric covers old blue fabric on the chairs.

sunny
elegance

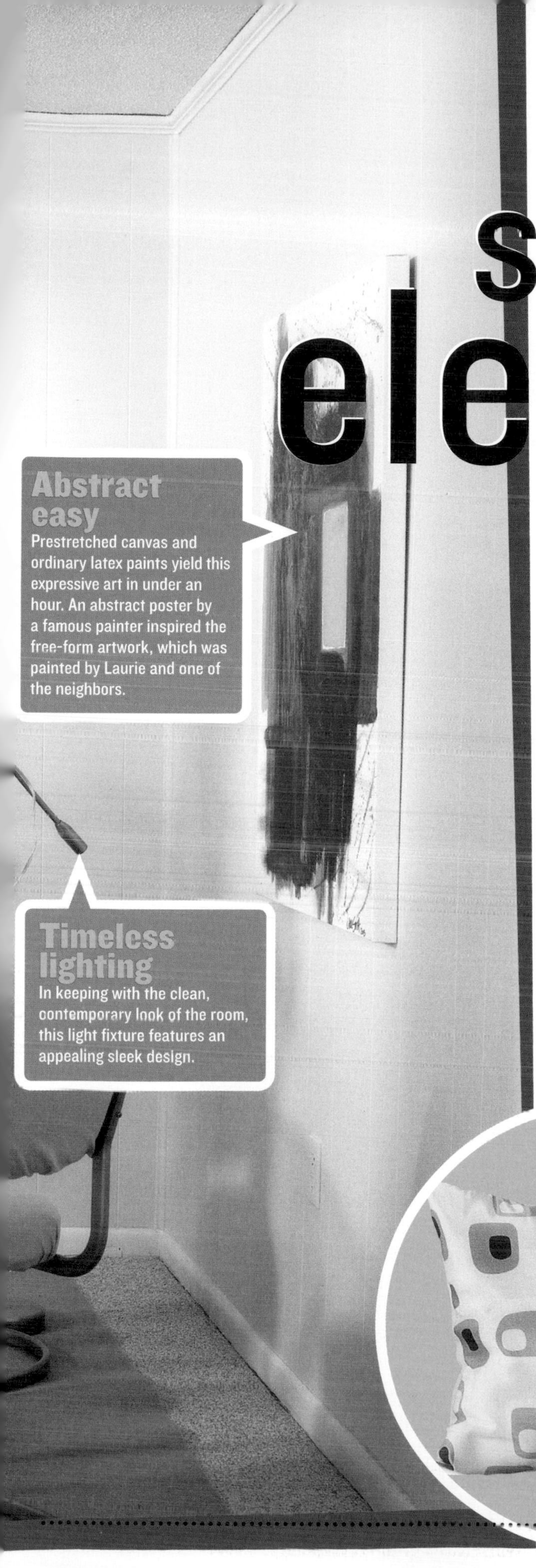

Abstract easy

Prestretched canvas and ordinary latex paints yield this expressive art in under an hour. An abstract poster by a famous painter inspired the free-form artwork, which was painted by Laurie and one of the neighbors.

Timeless lighting

In keeping with the clean, contemporary look of the room, this light fixture features an appealing sleek design.

Open floor plans pose decorating dilemmas in many homes. Laurie answers the challenge in this living room by using soft, classic color and understated styling for furniture and accessories. Take a look too at the clever tactics for hiding a huge television and deciding where to stop and start paint color for the ceiling.

Fabric first

A single yard of funky geometric-print fabric sparked the color scheme of earthy yellows and browns.

▶Miami: Miami Place

The homeowners recognize that their living room pieces are mismatched. "This room needs help," one of them says. "We just want it to look a lot nicer and more uniform. We don't have a color scheme." Because the living room is open to the kitchen, Laurie faces some tough decisions on where to begin and end new features to ensure good visual flow.

The owners of this large living room are tired of their mismatched furnishings and long for a strong color scheme. They want a subtle, uniform look that will be elegant without seeming stuffy. Because the living room is open to the kitchen, good visual flow between the rooms is also important to them.

Laurie points out that the living room feels drab and needs some vibrancy. She starts with soft yellow for the walls. "We are going to bring some life into the room with a little bit of color," she says. "But we are going to make it tone-on-tone so it is going to appear neutral." Choosing yellow in different shades will help Laurie achieve the monochromatic look she's after.

An earthy yellow-brown hue, which Laurie dubs "acorn," ties the ceiling into the new color palette and brings warmth to the setting. The key decision was where to stop and start color because the ceiling over the living room flows into the adjoining kitchen. Moldings added to the ceiling offer an easy solution by providing boundaries for the paint, creating a rectangle of color like an area rug overhead.

◄ Save time deciding on a color palette by starting with a piece of fabric and using it as a guide. Laurie had only one yard of the geometric pattern shown on the pillow on the left. She used the fabric to make three pillow fronts and then used plain fabric for the backs.

time crunch

► entertainment centers

If you opt not to build an entertainment center because of time constraints, consider commandeering an existing closet to store your audiovisual equipment. Or use wood or wire closet components to create storage for media equipment on a wall or in an alcove. Here are some other options to consider:

► **ADAPT FURNITURE** Laurie once used an old chest of drawers to store a television. She removed the two upper drawers and divider to create a TV-size opening. You could also retrofit the kneehole of an old desk with a shelf to hold a stereo or television; the drawers can store CDs and DVDs. Set a DVD player or VCR on the desktop.

► **ASSEMBLE CUBES** Most discount stores and home centers carry cube-type storage that is easy to assemble. Combine the cubes into configurations to suit your needs. Stack them on the floor or hang them from the walls.

► **COMBINE CUBES AND WOOD PANELS** Stack wide panels of ¾-inch-thick wood with storage cubes or stack them on glass blocks (the type used for windows or transparent dividing walls). Don't use particleboard for shelves because it isn't strong enough. Use aspen, pine, or oak panels, which are available at home centers in a variety of widths and lengths.

◄ Sometimes mistakes can actually improve a room. Laurie accidentally broke the first light fixture she purchased. Luckily, she liked this sleek new one even better.

► Laurie originally considered laying new carpeting in the living room. However, she noted that the existing carpeting was glued down and "would be a nightmare to take out." Laying a new swath of carpeting on the old—like an extra large area rug—freshens the space in record time.

From the Designers

►LAURIE HICKSON SMITH

Q What items do you always have on hand in your decorating pantry?

A A quart of trim paint. Children with their toys—and even adults at dinner parties—can easily nick your doors, cabinets, and trim. Keep paint on hand and use it like white out.

Interesting vases in shapes and colors that you love. It's amazing how your whole mood can change when you walk into a room with fresh flowers on the coffee table. And having a collection of vases nearby entices you to have fresh flowers more often.

Q If you had only one afternoon to refresh the look of a room, what would you do?

A Rearrange the furniture. I tell people to "pull a *Trading Spaces*"—empty out the room, order pizza, and have some bonding time. Ask yourself how things would look in a different location. Find a new focal point. Try an asymmetrical look for a while. Set furniture up on the diagonal. Just experiment.

Q What are some fabulous artwork ideas for people who think they have no time or talent?

A Get a canvas and splatter paint on it. You'll have a fabulous, dramatic piece. If you're not comfortable with canvas, try poster board. If you don't like paint, upholster wood pieces with batting and funky fabric. Just have fun with it. Or simply paint stripes on your walls. Anyone can do a straight line. Experiment with combinations of color and make the stripes your artistic statements.

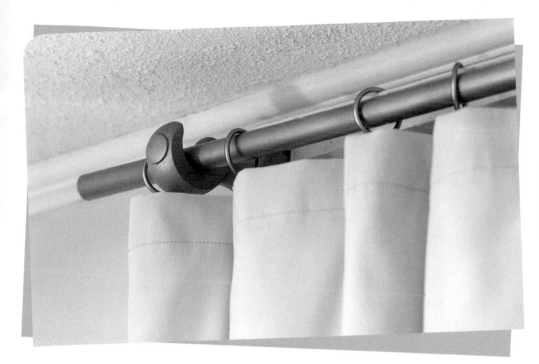

◀ Fabric for the window treatments matches fabric used to slipcover the futon, enhancing the unity of the space. Make curtain panels in a snap by using fusible webbing to create hems. Hang the panels from clip-on rings threaded onto a rod.

Because the living room is long, it easily divides into two activity areas when the furnishings are grouped according to function: a conversation area for relaxing and watching television and a dining area.

In the conversation area, building a closet with sliding doors provides a place to hide a large-screen television. Wood paneling covers drywall used to construct the new closet sidewall, so the addition blends seamlessly with the existing wood paneling on the surrounding walls. For stylish seating, a slipcover in a rich golden brown refreshes the futon, which teams with an affordable pair of modern-style wicker chairs.

For the dining area, Laurie reuses an old dining set, updating the totally '80s brass tubing with chrome spray paint and refreshing the chair seats with soft yellow fabric. The dining area also functions as a mini art gallery: Narrow shelving provides a place for matted and framed family photos, and an adjacent wall displays an abstract painting created by one of the neighbors.

The final result is one elegant room with a variety of functions—all wrapped in warm, inviting color.

◀ Classic shelves like these can be found online and in catalogs, preassembled and ready to install.

what you need

Materials
Two 4-foot-long ledges
  or shelves (available
  through catalogs,
  discount stores, and
  home centers)
Empty frames
Candleholders
Taper candles

Tools
Screwdriver
Carpenter's level
Pencil

shelf discovery

One big landscape painting above the sofa is a perennial choice for living room artwork. Branch out a bit and express yourself more creatively with shelves. You'll need only a few hours, a couple of streamlined shelves, and a collection of frames and candles.

1. **Start** by using a carpenter's level to lightly pencil an 8-foot-long horizontal line onto the wall. Choose a height and position that relates well to the furnishings in the room.

2. **Align** the shelves with the pencil mark and screw them to the wall using the brackets or devices provided by the manufacturer.

3. **Arrange** the empty frames, creating a focal point slightly to the right or left of center in the total arrangement. To unify mismatched frames, choose one or two metallic or matte finishes and spray-paint all the frames. Add candleholders, candles, vases, and other items, arranging them in clusters or in one strong grouping.

scissors

Quality scissors dramatically simplify the job when you're doing a lot of cutting. Lengths range from 5 to 13 inches; the larger models typically weigh more, so choose a pair that suits your hand size and strength. Choose steel-blade models for lasting sharpness and look for ergonomically designed padded handles for extra comfort.

Before you leave the store, take the scissors out of the package and open and close the blades several times to see if the tension feels comfortable. (Some models offer an adjustable pivot that lets you modify the blade tension to your liking.) Plan to keep three or four pairs in your decorating pantry:

▶ **CRAFTING SCISSORS** Available at crafts and office supply stores, these scissors are a great all-around choice. They're perfect for all paper crafts, from decoupage to scrapbooking.

▶ **SEWING SCISSORS** Designed with fabric cutting in mind, these ultrasharp scissors typically feature offset handles for easier cutting along flat surfaces. Sewing scissors are available at fabric and crafts stores.

▶ **PINKING SHEARS** Also available at fabric and crafts stores, these scissors offer a zigzag cut to reduce fabric raveling. Pinking shears can also be used to add a decorative zigzag edge to embellishments made from fabric scraps, felts, and papers.

▶ **DECORATIVE-EDGE SCISSORS** Similar to pinking shears and available at the same places, these scissors are designed to cut a repetitive pattern and one perfect for adding edge detailing to fabrics, felts, and papers. Several different cutting patterns are available, including smooth scallops, flowing waves, and various combinations of angles and curves.

Over the top

The center of the ceiling matches the wall color; for interest, color outside the ceiling molding is one shade darker.

Faux focus

Installing an authentic fireplace requires time and a good chunk of money. Building this false fireplace out of MDF produced a focal point in 48 hours.

Tile style

Boasting the look of more costly wood parquet tiles, the tiles facing the fireplace are actually peel-and-stick vinyl.

Warm attraction

The walls started out cool Key lime green. Fresh coats of camel make the room feel more warm and inviting.

Material matters

Tone-on-tone fabric replaces a country print on the chairs for a more traditional look.

focal point favorite

New heights

These custom-built wood pedestals feature clear tops that allow uplights to shine through and highlight tall urns. Vertical elements such as these help draw the eye upward.

Urn cache

A ginger jar fits the theme of traditional elegance. This type of accessory can be found at import stores and online.

Classic black

Stained-wood end tables and the coffee table are painted black, and other black accents are introduced to create elegance.

A high ceiling and attractive moldings gave this former home office space a good beginning, yet it lacked a focal point. Using unexpected materials, Edward devises a fashionable feature that draws the eye, and he warms up the walls with cheerful, sunny color. Finally, Edward adds his trademark touch: a few elegant black accents.

A small study in a house can be a bonus or a bust, depending on whether household members enjoy being in the space. The family residing in this house admitted that their study wasn't welcoming. "You don't want to go in there and hang out," says one young family member. "It would be nice If we could go in there and hang out and not worry about messing something up."

Edward sees one of the problems: "Right now, this room has very little function," he says. "I want to make it into something they can use for socializing and reading."

He starts by warming up the walls with camel color, carrying the hue onto the ceiling and adding a mat of darker camel outside the existing molding on the ceiling.

Although the room is tall, it's also square and lacks architectural character. Edward introduces a false fireplace—constructed of MDF—and adds a facade of peel-and-stick vinyl tiles in a wood parquet pattern. Painting the firebox and hearth black makes the structure more elegant. Extra deep crown moldings are left white to stand out against the camel walls.

Existing furnishings receive makeovers too, starting with a pair of stained-wood coffee tables, which Edward paints black. Two armchairs look dressier with new tone-on-tone ivory fabric that covers a dated country print. An ivory corduroy slipcover conceals old fabric on the sofa.

Floor-to-ceiling cream draperies, a graphic painting, and a pair of classic urns on lighted pedestals round out the makeover. The finished space seems to please Edward as much as it pleases the homeowners:

"This is the room closest to my true personality and style," Edward says. "It's my favorite room."

before

►**North Carolina: Dogwood Trail**

Barren walls the color of Key lime pie make this study feel cold and unfriendly. Sparse furnishings don't lend themselves to much use. "You don't want to go in there and spend time," says one of the homeowners' daughters. In this *Trading Spaces Family* episode, Mom is hoping for a desk for doing homework and working on the computer.

◄ For this window treatment, no rod pockets are needed. Cut fabric long enough to loop over the top of the rod and secure with ribbon or decorative cord and tassels. If you prefer not to sew hems, use iron-on fusible webbing to secure the hems. For more information on fusible webbing, see page 45.

time crunch

▶ instant work spaces

Edward found a fast way to create a desk for the study, *left,* using a split column for legs and an MDF panel for the top. Consider these other ideas when you need a work space fast:

▶ **SAWHORSE SOLUTIONS**
Set up a pair of wood or metal sawhorses and top them with a solid-core door or a prefabricated ¾-inch wood panel (made for shelves). Finish as desired.

▶ **FILING FOUNDATION**
Use a pair of two-drawer filing cabinets to support a desk top.

▶ **TRAY TRANSFORMATION**
To create a writing surface that you can put away, fashion a slipcover to cover a television tray and make it more attractive. Use a dining chair for a seat.

▶ **WAKE-UP CALL** If you need to work when you're down with a cold (or you merely want to work from the most comfortable place in your home!), equip a bed tray set with a calculator, pens, and paper. Store the tray under a bedside table so it's accessible.

From the Designers

▶ EDWARD WALKER

Q What were some of your favorite aspects of this room redo?

A I liked that it had very clean lines. It was traditional but with some modern aspects to it. It was functional as well as comfortable. The arrangement of the sofa and chairs made it possible to relax and converse. The desk off to the side for the computer was wonderful too. It could be used as a bar to have drinks at or to serve hors d'oeuvres when entertaining.

Q If you had only one afternoon to refresh a room, what would you do?

A I definitely would move the furniture out of the room and really think about placement of it. I'd invest in some window treatments—a new valance or pair of drapes on the window. I'd then maybe pick up a couple of new throw pillows and a couple of new lamps.

If I couldn't go out shopping, I would look around the house and see if there is something that would work better furniturewise. For example, look in the basement or the garage—that dresser somebody gave you that you didn't know what to do with—it may be a great entry table in the foyer or a great side table.

Q When you're shopping, what's the biggest time-waster—and how do you avoid it?

A Probably not having a plan. When I shop for myself, I take along a design folder. I use just simple manila folders; I paint my wall color on the inside and attach little fabric samples from the sofa, throw pillows, and so on.

Make sure you also have room dimensions written down. That way, if you're looking at a certain piece, you can refer to the wall dimensions and you'll know if it will fit. Include window sizes as well, so when you see a great deal on curtain rods, you'll know right away if they will fit.

I also make notes in the folder: blue vase, such-and-such store, on June 6, and $20. Then two weeks later or whenever I'm ready to purchase, I can look at my folder and recall where it was and how much.

▶ Peel-and-stick vinyl tiles make surfacing a false fireplace a snap.

▼ Slipcovering a chair like this one requires patience. Decorative tack strips—such as the one shown around the arm—can speed the process. The strip features faux tacks joined together with intermittent holes to accept real tacks, so you'll only have to drive in a small number to secure the fabric.

candles

Candlelight warms the ambience of a room better than any other light source. Top your tables with a plethora of pillars, votives, and tapers to bring a welcoming and warming glow to any gathering.

When filling a traditional candelabra, choose tapers of the same color and width and in heights that complement the holder. Mix and match candles in individual holders, using tapers or pillars of varying colors and widths to complement your decor and your mood. Scented candles can further enhance the atmosphere; however, avoid using them when you are serving dinner—they can interfere with the aroma of the meal.

Although smokeless, dripless candles can cost two or three times more than standard discount store varieties. However, they are worth the extra cost when you plan to use them on the dining table or sideboard or in hanging fixtures or wall sconces. These candles reduce the amount of smoke in the air and eliminate wax drips that can damage table linens and floor coverings. (Note: Even dripless candles can drip a bit when a draft or breeze is present.) Dripless, smokeless candles are available in some specialty candle shops and on the Internet (type "dripless smokeless candles" in the search field of your favorite search engine). Here are two ways to decorate with candles:

▶ **CREATE AN INSTANT CENTERPIECE** by topping a footed glass cake stand with three or four pillar candles, choosing one or two colors and a variety of heights. Space the candles in a pleasing arrangement on the plate and then fill in around the candles with clear- or colored-glass florist's pebbles (flat on one side), available at crafts and home decor stores.

▶ **TOP YOUR COFFEE TABLE** with a varied assortment of candleholders, then fill the holders with various heights and widths of candles all in one color to create a look that is both unified and unique.

▲ A custom-made slipcover makes the sofa look like new. If you don't have time or skills to sew your own slipcovers, check online and in catalogs for ready-made covers that fit beautifully and offer updated styles.

◀ Artwork doesn't have to take hours and hours to create. For the checkerboard design on this canvas, Edward painted a black background and then asked each family member to paint a square. The top coat of color is thin to allow some of the black background to show through. The neighbors who painted the piece signed and dated it as a fond memory.

magnificent mantels

Arranging a mantel is all about assembling a group of items in an attractive way. For quick mantel decor, choose from formal (and symmetrical) or informal (and asymmetrical) styles. For faster results, use only one kind of object; a mix of items often requires more experimentation for good results.

These two demonstrations use classic mantel collections—clocks and mirrors. Follow these steps:

what you need

In an hour

Materials
One large focal
  point item
Even numbers of
  medium-size items
Small items
Optional: Pedestals, such
  as blocks or books

Formal finesse

Symmetrical, or formal, arrangements are easier than asymmetrical because you arrange equal-size objects in the same manner on each side of a central axis.

1. **Gather** items of the same type, such as clocks, mirrors, pictures, plates, or empty antique frames.

2. **Practice** the arrangement on the floor in front of the mantel to get a sense of how it will come together on the mantel. Eliminate items that don't fit into the plan. Note the amount of space the collection takes up. Plan comfortable spaces between items (not too small and not too big).

3. **Center** and hang the large focal point item above the mantel. Position the focal point piece high enough to allow placement of items below.

4. **Hang** medium-size objects on the wall, balancing the number and sizes equally on each side of the focal point.

5. **Arrange** small items along the mantel, raising them on pedestals, if desired, for additional interest. Remember to balance the number and size of smaller items equally on each side of the central axis.

formal.....

informal...

Artistically asymmetrical

Arranging a mantel collection informally requires more confidence than formal arranging. If you want to create a more casual feel, this style is for you. Trust your sense of what feels balanced and what doesn't. Work with odd-numbered, one-of-a-kind objects. If possible, include a pair of matched items. In this process, you'll add and subtract until everything "feels" right. You'll get the best results if you vary the sizes and select one special object to play a focal point role. Follow these guidelines as you work:

1. **Collect** a group of items with the same theme. For ease in rearranging, choose a set of flat objects, such as mirrors, pictures, or empty frames, which can lean rather than hang on the wall above the mantel. This layering method adds to the flexibility of informal arranging: You can rearrange any time your mood changes or the season requires a different theme. You can also avoid marring the wall.

2. **Choose** one or two large items for the first layer against the wall. Overlap two if they're too large for the mantel width or use two to make the background layer large enough to frame the rest of the pieces.

3. **Add** a second layer. A matching pair of objects will quickly bring stability and balance to an informal arrangement. You can also successfully achieve the second layer with unmatched pieces that work well together and provide a background for the focal point item.

4. **Finish** with the focal point (the most interesting item in the collection) by placing it slightly to the left or right of center. The perfect focal point place, sometimes known as "the golden mean," is one-third of the way across the mantel from either direction.

Tactile pleasures
Joint compound troweled onto walls adds another pleasing dimension to the room.

Bold beginning
Deep red paint topped with a walnut glaze provides librarylike elegance. The glaze creates the illusion of an aged finish by muting the color intensity. The darker glaze settles in the depressions, giving the illusion of deeper texture.

study in red

DESIGNED BY CHRISTI

Old house interiors don't have to look dowdy. Christi steps in and shows how to instill a lively look in the study of a 130-year-old home without covering its charming character. Texture and rich red paint transform walls while a pair of desks teams up with plenty of new shelves to make this space both beautiful and functional.

Shelf discovery
Though the designers often use painted MDF to save money, investing extra dollars in those hardwood veneer shelves allows a dark stain finish, which plays up the Old World library ambience.

Salvage bonus
Decorative balusters, which were purchased from a salvage yard, support the shelves and call attention to the vintage theme of the room.

A pair of wings
Yet another salvage purchase, the wing chairs feature traditional styling that suits the era of the house. Slipcovers update the chairs in virtually no time.

Work ethic
This desk (a matching one is on the opposite wall) features a wood-veneer to continue the venerable dark stain.

Feet first
A red cushion dresses up this existing storage coffee table and pulls the wall color to the center of the room.

▶before

Unlike many "before" rooms on *Trading Spaces,* there was much that the owners appreciate about this study, which is located in a home that is more than a century old. "It's a comforting room with a nice view and a sunny south exposure," one owner says. "It's a nice place to do work and not be stressed out." The couple loves the fireplace as well as the inherent charm of the room; they're hoping Christi will

◀ A $3 box of salvaged tiles yields a handsome new hearth for the fireplace. Rather than spend hours chipping off the old grout from the tiles, Christi dug through the box and used only the cleanest tiles.

use her design expertise to play up the best features of the space. Because the couple read and work in this room, they're also hoping for shelves. Christi agrees and also plans more ideas that will yield an elegant Old World library look.

Sanding down portions of the existing white paint on the wood trim throughout the room creates an appealing illusion of wear and age. Christi then works with the neighbors to add texture to the walls by slathering joint compound onto the surfaces with trowels. "This brings in some good movement," she says.

Although fans blow on the new wall finish throughout the night, the surfaces are still slightly damp in the morning. Time is running short, however, and the painting must be done. Christi selects a deep ruby red paint that offers a dramatic contrast to the white woodwork. Applying glaze tinted with walnut stain over the dry paint dials down the newness of the color and adds a dark, aged patina that suits the old house.

time crunch

▶ shelves in minutes

Bring order to piles of books and photos by creating your own shelves in a flash:

▶ **BLOCKBUSTER STYLE.** Take a cue from dorm-room days and add an elegant twist. Stack dimensional lumber or prefabricated shelves on glass blocks resting on the floor. Add additional blocks as separators between shelves.

▶ **BRACKET BONUS.** Home centers, catalogs, and online sources offer a wide variety of decorative bracket styles. Hang the brackets on the walls and use them to support shelves made of wood or glass.

▶ **BOXED BEAUTY.** Flea markets are a fruitful source of old wood boxes or crates that can add an attractive vintage touch to any room. Secure the bottom of the box flat against the wall for the sides to serve as the shelves.

▶ **BASKET CASES.** Hang a collection of wicker or wire baskets, bottoms flat against the wall, to serve as stylish woven shelves.

▶ **DRAWER DYNAMICS.** Pull the drawers out of a has-been flea market dresser and hang them on the wall as shelves. Either secure the bottom of the drawer flat against the wall, or secure the back of the drawer to the wall with the bottom facing up to serve as a shelf.

◀ Rather than take time to make your own artwork, consider alternatives such as this vintage tin tile. Discovered at a salvage yard and hung above the fireplace, the tile now serves as three-dimensional art.

◀◀ Velvety red and gold fabric covers a new cushion for this storage piece that doubles as an ottoman. Make fast work of this project by topping a base with a thick foam cushion and laying fabric over the cushion. Staple the edges of the fabric to the base and hide staples by applying decorative cord or fringe with hot glue.

◄ The owners already loved the look of their fireplace; sanding the paint for a worn look and painting the surrounding walls bright red helps make it a focal point. Using an orbital or palm sander makes it easy to recreate a similar aged look on painted finishes in your house.

◄◄ Shelves hung directly on the walls above the desk free up floor space and provide an abundance of space for books and display. Crumbling plaster-over-lathe construction made installing these shelves a time-consuming project. If your home is stud-frame construction, you can save time installing shelves by finding studs first with a stud finder—a device available at home centers. Screw shelves directly to the studs for a secure installation.

Old tiles in varying shades of white, discovered at a salvage yard for $3 for an entire boxful, transform a plain wood hearth.

Christi takes advantage of two opposing walls by adding oak-veneer desktops and shelves that stretch across the width of the wall and to the ceiling. Choosing real wood veneer instead of less-expensive MDF to build the desks and shelves allows Christi to choose a dark, elegant stained finish for these pieces—a better fit for the library look.

A pair of wing chairs, purchased from a salvage place, gain new slipcovers and prominent positions at the center of the room. Paired with a cushioned storage ottoman, the chairs offer comfortable and attractive seating for reading.

Artwork is always a smart way to finish a space, and Christi makes an apropos choice by hanging a vintage tin ceiling tile on the diagonal above the fireplace.

"This is my style too, I think," Christi says with a smile.

From the Designers

▶ CHRISTI PROCTOR

Q My bookshelves are overflowing with stuff. What tips do you suggest for rearranging items so my displays look more attractive and organized?

A Cut out the things that are not essential. Thin it out and use more layering with your stuff. Turn books on their sides and place decorative objects on them. Apply fabric or wallpaper to the backs of the bookcases to give them some life.

Q I get bored quickly with the look of my rooms. Could you offer some ideas for quickly changing the look on a whim?

A Slipcovers!!! Have a couple of options for the seasons that blend with the permanent things, such as your wall paint.

Q Fabric stores are great, but generally speaking where else can I go to get exceptional deals on fabric?

A Try to find the warehouse districts in larger cities. I buy almost all of my fabrics for the show in huge places that are stocked floor-to-ceiling.

In a few hours

what you need

Materials

Cluttered bookcase
Focal point accents,
  such as finials or
  photographs
Similar collections,
  such as white
  stoneware pitchers
Books
Plants/flowers
Comfy chair for
  reading
Artwork for
  surrounding walls

Tools

Pliers, to pull shelf-
  support tabs out
  and reposition
  shelves

bookcase shape-up

Bookcases—either built-in or freestanding—are a terrific bonus in any home. Unfortunately, they can become cluttered and chaotic. If you've been avoiding editing the things on your bookshelves—wondering where to begin and where it will all end—follow these quick tips for making your shelves shipshape with only a minimal investment in time.

B.

A.

C.

Select a bookcase or bookcases in your home. Transform the look and function of the cases with the following steps:

1. Pack away small items to reduce clutter. (Or if your bookcase has lower cabinets, such as this one, *left*, use them for storing small or unattractive items.) Keep a theme to what you place on the shelves by repeating objects, such as books and baskets teamed with vintage items and minimal color.

2. Reposition the shelves to create a larger opening at the center. This area serves as a focal point, drawing your eye's attention first and then letting your eye travel to other groupings. (For example, rustic finials lure the eye to the center bookshelf in Photo A.)

3. Group similar objects in odd numbers for balance and greater impact.

4. Select pretty boxes and other storage containers, such as baskets (see Photo B) or bins, to hold less attractive objects—CDs and paperback books, for example.

5. Create layers. Arrange items in front-to-back layers as well as top-to-bottom layers. When layering objects of different heights and sizes, avoid overcrowding. Allow space between objects so each can be seen and appreciated.

6. Play with height. Stacks of books and boxes provide height for displaying objects (see Photo C).

7. Introduce softness by including curved objects in some of the vignettes. Plants, flowers, and other natural elements add texture and color. Keep arrangements grounded by placing visually weighty objects on lower shelves.

8. Finish the look. The area around a bookcase is important too. Place a comfy chair or bench nearby for reading. Hang artwork or photographs on the walls.

the decorating pantry

fabrics

You don't have to spend a lot of money on fabric to give your rooms a new look. For makeovers in minutes, keep these three fabrics on hand:

▶ **MUSLIN** This inexpensive 100-percent-cotton fabric is available in two colors, natural and white, and in widths from 36 to 120 inches. Prices range from $2 to $10 per yard, depending on width. The cloth is ideal for quilt backings, curtain panels, slipcovers, or table linens.

▶ **FAUX SUEDE** This 100-percent-polyester material is available in a range of colors that look and feel like actual suede but cost about one-third as much. (Suede retails for as much as $45 per yard, while faux suede retails for less than $15 per yard.) The synthetic material is stain-resistant and doesn't ravel, so it's a perfect choice for making no-sew place mats, table runners, or desk pads. You can also staple the material over an old ottoman or chair pad for new style.

▶ **FELT** Available by the yard and in precut squares, this 100-percent-polyester material is available in nearly every color and serves as an excellent problem solver. Retailing for less that $3 per yard, this nonraveling, nappy material is ideal for appliqués and makes a perfect buffer: Use it under vases, pottery, lamps, bed frames, and audiovisual equipment to prevent dents and scratches in freshly painted or stained surfaces.

ring around
the room

Worth repeating
The Os repeated on the walls were created quickly with a stamp.

Unity matters
Though the end table and sofa have different styling, their shared paint color unifies the look.

Sofa saver
Fabric and fresh paint update a thrift store sofa. The soft taupe material adds subtle color yet allows the repeating pattern to remain the focus of the room.

DESIGNED BY HILDI

Storage island
Rather than clutter the walls with bookshelves, Hildi designed a three-piece storage unit that sits in the center of the room for easy access. Wheels allow each unit to roll where needed.

Because this oversize family room serves as a home school during the day, the homeowners are hoping Hildi will provide storage for their vast collection of books and supplies. They would also like the space to be more accommodating for adult gatherings.

Low-cost flooring
Some savvy shopping at a home center yielded enough carpet to redo the room for about $250—or 5l cents per square foot.

▲ One quiet corner accommodates a small desk for the computer. A white lamp with a black shade adds style.

▶ Paint updates the table and four chairs, and matching fabric pulls the seats into the playful circle theme. Creating a lot of artwork wasn't necessary for this makeover—the walls are the art.

This supersize family room is the perfect space for the owners to homeschool their children. However, the couple admits that—aside from school hours—they aren't motivated to spend much time here. They want the room to be better organized; they're also hoping it can become an inviting gathering place for adults and kids alike.

As the room decorating gets under way, a snag occurs. Like most houses, this one has a hidden problem: water damage below a window. No matter the time limits, it's essential to address any structural harm to a house, and Hildi knows it. New 2×4s and sheathing are installed, and decorating begins with a fresh coat of off-white paint over all the walls and the ceiling. Using a sprayer

▶**before**

▶Miami: Miami Place

This family room, which functions as a home school during weekdays, is huge. The family who lives here wants to spend more relaxing hours in the room. "But right now we don't," says one homeowner, "because the kids have taken over. It's not friendly to adults, so we really want a mixture for adults and kids."

makes this phase of the project go faster. The walls are then treated to an allover pattern that continues the look of the fabric Hildi has chosen for the window treatments and chair covers.

Though the homeowners and neighbors say they favor bright colors, Hildi opts for an abundance of pattern in neutral tones instead. "People think they want a lot of color because it stimulates their minds," Hildi says. "But the pattern actually does the same thing."

To furnish the room, Hildi turns to secondhand furniture, including a sofa, tall stools, and a dining table; the four existing chairs were previously scattered throughout the room. After everything is sanded, primer, taupe paint, and new fabrics give

▶ high-speed repeating patterns

A handmade stamp eased the process of covering these walls with a repeating pattern. Stamps are also available at crafts stores to help you decorate your walls. Here are some other ideas for quick repeats:

▶ **IMPERFECT STRIPES** Rather than create perfect stripes with a carpenter's level and painter's tape, mark stripe widths across the top and bottom of the wall. Then start at the top of each stripe and pull a paintbrush or narrow-width roller downward. These imperfect stripes take less time than taped-off ones and offer a casual look.

▶ **KIDDIE COOL** For a fun look in a child's bedroom or bath, use finger painting! Have your children dip their hands in paint and press their palms to the wall for hand-shape patterns. Use different colors for an even bolder decor. This trick works with little feet too; lift up small children to have them stamp a playful path of painted footprints across the ceiling.

▶ **CUP CREATION** Create your own version of Os dancing across the walls. Dip the lips of plastic foam cups into paint and stamp on rings. For variety use different colors. Or introduce additional sizes using smaller paper cups or large plasticware bowls.

▶ **STENCIL STATEMENTS** You can never go wrong with the tried-and-true decorative standby—stencils. To keep the process quick, choose a one-layer stencil and stick with a single color of paint.

▶ **IMAGE CONSCIOUS** Purchase, rent, or borrow a crafts-quality opaque projector. To find an image you want to use on the wall, look to fabric, wrapping paper, or design books. Cast the pattern onto the wall with the opaque projector and use paint markers to trace the pattern. Fill the pattern in with paint or leave the outlines as they are.

each piece a fresh beginning. New plywood circles are cut for the stools; the plywood is topped with cushions and fabric.

Having established an inviting scheme for the room, Hildi turns to the question of storage. Her solution is a group of custom-built wedge-shape shelves that can sit in the middle of the room and be accessed from all sides. Although Hildi originally envisioned four wedge-shape pieces that would come together like a pie, the quarters wouldn't fit through the door. Ty had just enough time to rebuild three of the units. Casters let the units move wherever they may be needed around the room.

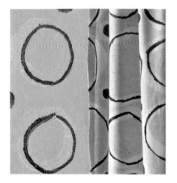

▲ Using a sprayer to paint all the walls off-white made the job go faster. Though the neighbors had to make numerous Os to cover the new background, they simplified the job by using a handmade stamp—a circle cut from a sponge and glued to a board. White circles were stamped on first and allowed to dry. Black circles were painted on freehand.

▶ These barstools, primed and painted by Hildi's team, were a thrift store find. No matter how pressed you are for time, take time for a primer coat. Primer acts like a glue for your top coat, reducing the possibility of chips and nicks and decreasing the number of paint coats required. Primers also prevent grease, smoke, and water stains from penetrating through to the top coat. Before you apply primer, check that the surface is clean and dry and that all flaky, loose paint has been scraped and brushed away.

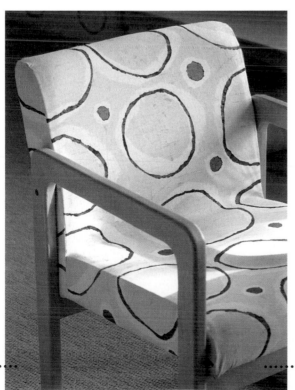

▲ This island storage unit was built from scratch. To create a similar unit in less time, purchase a pair of same-size shelving units, secure them back-to-back with screws, and add casters to the bottom.

◄ Using a sprayer to paint this chair frame and other furniture helped speed the painting process.

one wow wall

what you need

Materials
White paint (base coat)
1 quart each of five
  interior latex paint
  colors (five shades
  of yellow are shown
  here)

Tools
Pencil
Measuring tape
Long straightedge
Carpenter's level
1-inch-wide painter's
  tape
Paintbrush or roller

If you want to make a different and dramatic statement with paint, consider this multicolor horizontal band approach. Painter's tape, a carpenter's level, and one or two helpers make the job doable in a day. To translate the project into any of your favorite colors, choose a paint strip that's banded in colors graduating from light to dark. Select a total of five shades from one or two strips and buy a quart of paint in each color. (Purchase the paint in gallons if you're painting an especially large room or selecting deep, rich colors.)

Note: These instructions are for standard, 8-foot-high walls. Adjust stripe widths to accommodate the height of your room.

1. **Base coat the walls white** for a crisp look. Let dry 48 hours. With a pencil and measuring tape, mark the wall in several places 22 inches from the floor. With a carpenter's level and long straightedge (or use an extra long level, if

A.

you own one), join the markings to form a level line the length of the wall.

2. **Fasten painter's tape** along the pencil line, aligning the bottom edge of the tape on

the line. Run your fingernail along the edge of the tape to prevent paint from bleeding underneath.

3. **Mark the wall** 16½ inches above the top edge of the first line of painter's tape. Draw a level line and align painter's tape with this line as in Step 2. Repeat two more times to prepare the last three bands for painting. Note that the top band of color will be slightly wider than the middle three bands.

4. **Paint the bands** with a paintbrush or roller, applying a different color to each of the taped-off bands (see Photo A). Start at the top of the wall, using the lightest color, and proceed downward, graduating to the darkest color at the bottom band. (Clean the brush or roller with water between colors or use fresh applicators.) Remove the tape before the paint dries (see Photo B).

B.

the decorating pantry

painting tools

When choosing between throwaway painting tools and quality ones, here is a good rule to go by: If cleanup will take longer than the painting, choose a disposable painting tool.

Available in many sizes, disposable sponge brushes are great for applying whitewash, decoupage medium, glass-etching cream, and crafts paint. The tapered tip on a sponge brush is good for getting into tight corners and crevices.

Disposable rollers are typically made with a cardboard inner roll. The roll will buckle when saturated, so you may be able to use the disposable roller for only a few hours of painting. These rollers are ideal for applying quick-drying glazes or oil-base primers.

When choosing quality paintbrushes instead of disposables, choose natural bristles for oil-base paints and synthetic bristles for water-base products. Look for a thick brush with secure bristles: Pull the bristles apart to see how many are actually in the brush and check to see if any of them are loose.

A quality roller features a solid core that feels firm and secure. Squeeze the roller to check for firmness as well as for loose fibers that might shed.

Like disposable brushes and rollers, the following painting tools will save you time:

▶ **DECORATIVE PAINTING KITS** contain everything you need to complete a decorative project, including brushes, various painting tools, base coats, and glazes. Step-by-step instructions help you achieve the desired results. Kits come in different sizes to match the size of your project, whether you're crackle-painting a small dresser or rag-rolling an entire family room.

▶ **PAINTER'S MITTS** look similar to car-washing mitts. They fit over your hand and are ideal for quickly painting spindles, wooden legs, or dining chairs. An interior liner protects your hand from the paint.

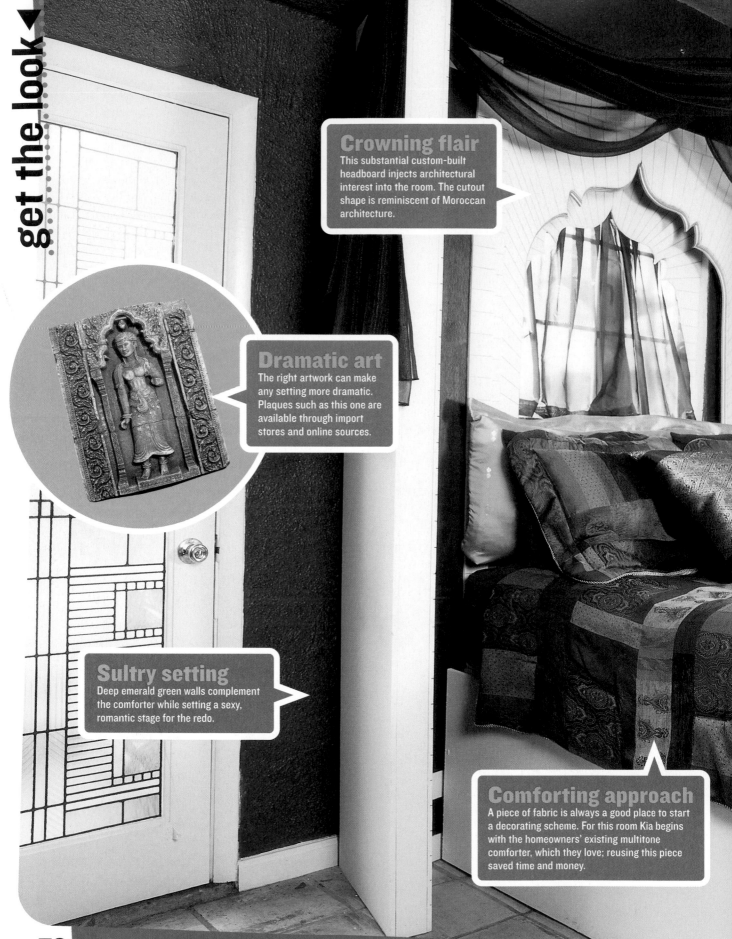

Crowning flair
This substantial custom-built headboard injects architectural interest into the room. The cutout shape is reminiscent of Moroccan architecture.

Dramatic art
The right artwork can make any setting more dramatic. Plaques such as this one are available through import stores and online sources.

Sultry setting
Deep emerald green walls complement the comforter while setting a sexy, romantic stage for the redo.

Comforting approach
A piece of fabric is always a good place to start a decorating scheme. For this room Kia begins with the homeowners' existing multitone comforter, which they love; reusing this piece saved time and money.

DESIGNED BY KIA

moroccan romance

Kia rises to the challenge when asked to incorporate an existing comforter into this bedroom makeover. The bed becomes a grand centerpiece, and layers of complementary jewel tones produce a space that's sexy, exotic, and sure to please the newlywed homeowners.

▶Orlando: Smith Street

An existing paver tile floor and a multicolor comforter, which the homeowners want to keep, give this master bedroom a good starting place. The owners don't like the stark white of the ceiling; they say they hope Kia will make the space "romantic, exotic, classic, peaceful, and calming."

▲ Glazed finishes, such as the one on this ceiling, lend pleasing dimension to a space and are easy to produce. Start with a light-color base coat, let dry, and then use damp rags or a roller to add a darker layer of glaze. Experiment with the richness of water-base glaze by adding one or two tablespoons at a time.

Not surprisingly, the newlywed homeowners use the words "romantic" and "peaceful" to describe the new look they'd like for their bedroom, and they label their white ceiling "boring." Somewhat unexpectedly, however, they ask if Kia could use their existing comforter.

Kia obliges on all counts. "We know she loves this bedspread," Kia says. "It's going to command our attention. We are going to use jewel tones—emeralds, topaz, rubies—all of those colors. We are going to do a magnificent bed, and it's going to be sexy. They are newlyweds, so we are going to make it hot!"

Dark emerald green paint on the walls adds sultry intrigue to the room; the boring white ceiling gains visual oomph with a two-

▶ door dress-ups . . . .

Doors are often-overlooked surfaces that are easy to embellish. Here are some ideas:

▶ **PAINT** Paneled doors at an entry or between rooms are good candidates for paint; so are recessed panels on cabinet doors. Consider painting panels with a contrasting color to make them stand out. Or use chalkboard paint, available in black or dark green, as a fun alternative. After the paint dries, use chalk to draw designs or write a message on the panels. Use a chalkboard eraser to wipe the panels clean.

▶ **DECOUPAGE** Paper images cut from a decoupage book or wallpaper can be applied to the door surface with decoupage medium.

▶ **ETCHING CREAM** See page 82 for ideas on using etching cream to create a design on glass door insets.

▼Stencils simplified the process of creating the intricate painted designs on this headboard. To make the billowy canopy, hang an extra long swath of sheer fabric over a rod installed perpendicular to the headboard wall. Drape the ends of the fabric over each side of the headboard.

▼A combination of paint and wallpaper yielded this elaborate column. If you can't find a wallpaper column, search for a similar image in a book. Use an opaque projector to cast the image onto the wall. Trace the image directly onto the wall in pencil or markers. Then fill in the outline with crafts paints or paint pens.

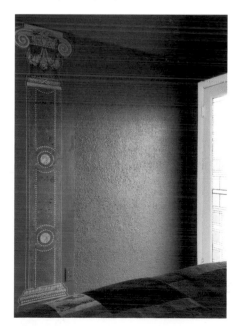

▶Moroccan style stirs up images of ancient objects, so it's fitting that this dresser is painted and sanded to look old. To do your own weathered finish, paint the furniture with a base coat color; let dry. Rub a candle on edges and other areas—anywhere that the furniture would wear naturally. Paint with a top coat color and let dry. Sand lightly wherever you applied candle wax to remove the topcoat color and reveal glimpses of the base coat.

etching cream

Available at crafts stores, etching cream can turn an ordinary piece of glass, whether it's colored or clear, into a work of art. In a few minutes, you can personalize gifts, customize stemware, or create beautiful borders on wall mirrors and window glass. To etch glass, clean the surface, dry thoroughly, and apply etching cream directly to the surface. Allow the cream to set according to manufacturer's directions—anywhere from a few seconds to a few minutes—then rinse with clear water. To create a design, apply the etching cream within a stencil. Here are a few great ways to add design dash to your home with the help of etching cream:

▸ **CREATE PRIVACY** in door sidelights or bathroom windows with heavily patterned geometric designs.

▸ **USE STENCILS** to create a floral pattern or monogram on the underside of a set of clear glass dinner plates. Make stemware and serving bowls to match.

▸ **DISGUISE SCRATCHES** and blemishes in mirrors by covering these problem areas with a hand-painted scroll and leaf pattern.

layer treatment of gold paint and dark gold glaze. Kia substitutes a wicker-blade ceiling fan for the old white one, giving the owners greater style—and remote control operation. Mirrored closet doors, which replace the plain panel versions, give the room a bit of glamour and help make the space appear larger and brighter.

The bed becomes a luxurious oasis, thanks to a 2-foot-high custom-built platform and a substantial curving headboard that nearly reaches the ceiling. A cutout in the center of the headboard reflects Kia's request for "Moroccan-style shrine architecture." The neighbors add intricate stencils to each side of the headboard to enhance the feeling of a faraway land. A filmy sheer panel the color of amethyst tops off the structure with a romantic flourish. More jewel tones appear behind the headboard, where new emerald green sheers filter light.

Kia saves money and time by reusing some of the homeowners' existing furniture, including a dresser that she decides to distress for a weathered look. Finishing the room is the beloved bedspread, which seems right at home in the new, sexier surroundings. Kia delights in the outcome at the end of the episode: "It is hot and spicy!" she exclaims.

From the Designers

▶ KIA STEAVE DICKERSON

Q What time-management strategies do you credit for your successes on the show?

A Paige Davis! My time-management strategy is to keep reminding myself, "Paige is coming, Paige is coming...."

Q What's one of your favorite areas of a home center to visit for decorating inspiration?

A The plumbing aisle has really cool things. There is so much you can do with pipe and plumbing accessories. I knew I wanted to make a chess set [for San Diego: Fairfield]. I lost sleep thinking about what I could do that would be unique. I wandered down the plumbing aisle, and all of a sudden, using plumbing pieces just struck me. And to think I was originally going to use wood dowels cut into shapes!

Q Is it a better investment of time and money to focus on one aspect (for example, wall color) of your entire home—or to focus solely on one room at a time?

A Focus on one room at a time. If you don't, you will kill yourself and you will drive your partner crazy. Don't take on a whole house unless you have a pro to map it out and you just won the lottery. Besides, no one wants their entire house disrupted. You need certain areas you can go to while you're renovating. Remodeling is serious business. You're making physical, financial, emotional, and mental investments. You need a certain place in your home that you can get away from all that sawdust and paint and just feel good and think clearly.

◀ Light filtering through the beautiful glass on this door gives more architectural interest to the room. If you have a glass-paned French door in your bedroom, give it the look of stained glass by applying adhesive-backed leading and stained-glass paints, available at crafts stores.

fast project ◀ inspired by the show

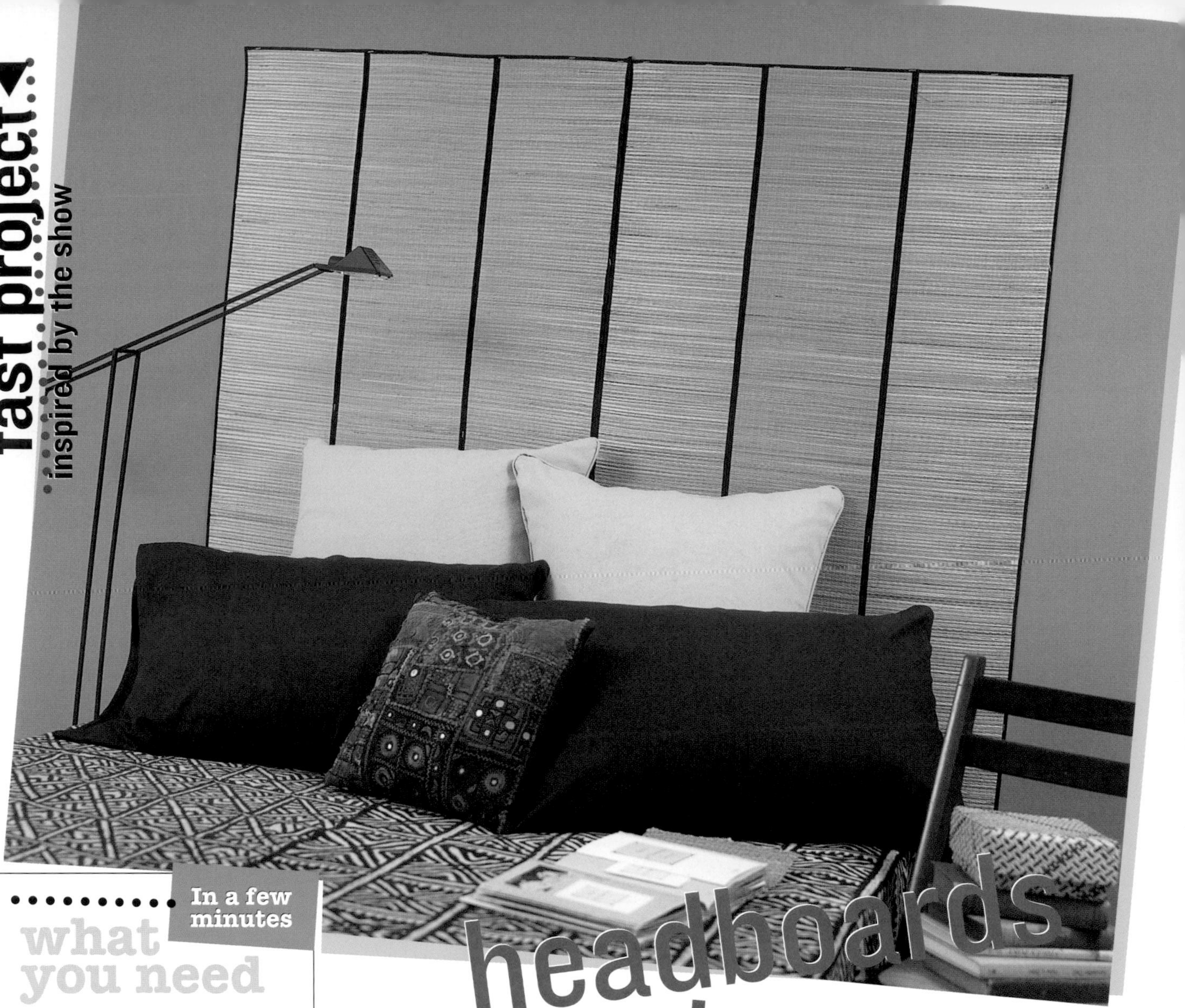

headboards in a hurry

An ordinary mattress and box spring become a fabulous focal point with either one of these superfast headboards. Fasten your chosen material to the wall and then step back and enjoy.

In a few minutes

what you need

BEACH BEAUTY

Materials

Two natural-grass beach mats with fabric-bound edges (available at import and swim supply stores)

Tools

Carpenter's level
Pencil
Staple gun
Staples

Beach beauty headboard

1. **Mark the center** of the bed on the wall above the head of the bed. Use a carpenter's level and a pencil to extend the mark in a vertical line; use this line as a guide for hanging the first mat. Use the carpenter's level and a pencil to draw a horizontal line above the bed to locate the top of the headboard.
2. **Position the first mat** by aligning one long edge with the vertical line and aligning the top edge with the horizontal line. Using a staple gun, staple the mat to the wall through the fabric-bound edges.
3. **Repeat** on the opposite side of the vertical line with the remaining mat. Fold up any excess length at the bottom of the mat and staple to the wall behind the bed.

what you need

COTTAGE CHIC

Materials

One 6×8-foot fence panel (available at lumberyards and by special order at home centers)

6-foot-long 1× or 2× board (to use as a nailing cleat to secure the fence to the wall; choose a board that matches the thickness of the horizontal rail on the back of the fence)

Tools

Palm sander
Sandpaper
Tack cloth
Stud finder
Handsaw, circular saw, or table saw
Carpenter's level
Measuring tape
Pencil
Cordless screwdriver
Long screws

Cottage chic headboard

1. **Trim excess pickets** from the fence panel on one side so it measures 78 inches wide for a king-size mattress, 67 inches wide for a queen-size bed, 62 inches wide for a full-size bed, and 40 inches wide for a twin-size bed. (Note that one 6×8-foot fence panel is large enough to make two twin-size headboards.) Use a palm sander and sandpaper to smooth the headboard. Wipe clean with a tack cloth.

2. **Mark the desired height** of the supporting cleat, using a measuring tape and pencil. (Position the top edge of the cleat so it will sit right below the bottom edge of the top rail on the back of the fence.) Use a carpenter's level and pencil to mark a horizontal line as a guide for the cleat. Center the line above the head of the bed.

3. **Use a stud finder** and pencil to mark the location of studs along the horizontal line. Align the cleat with the horizontal line and secure to wall studs with screws (see Photo A).

4. **Position the fence rail** so it rests on the top edge of the cleat. Secure the fence to the cleat by driving screws through the face of the fence and directly into the cleat (see Photo B).

A.

B.

Blue tranquility
Soft blue glaze applied to the walls and combed with a pick for a subtle strié makes this bedroom as peaceful as sunrise on the beach.

White refresher
Crisp white accents brighten the space and offer good contrast to blues used throughout the room.

DESIGNED BY FRANK

serene
sanctuary

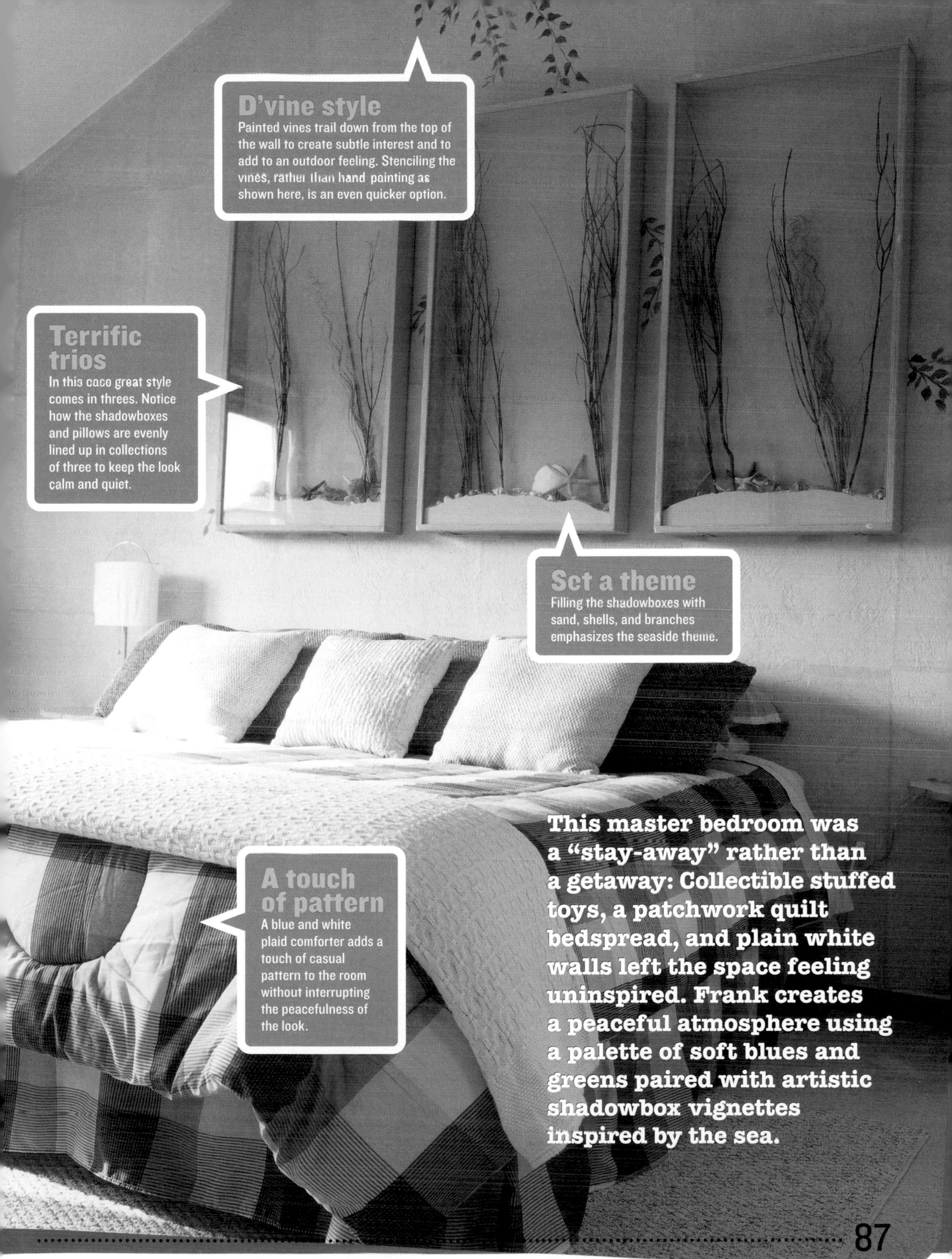

D'vine style

Painted vines trail down from the top of the wall to create subtle interest and to add to an outdoor feeling. Stenciling the vines, rather than hand painting as shown here, is an even quicker option.

Terrific trios

In this case great style comes in threes. Notice how the shadowboxes and pillows are evenly lined up in collections of three to keep the look calm and quiet.

Set a theme

Filling the shadowboxes with sand, shells, and branches emphasizes the seaside theme.

A touch of pattern

A blue and white plaid comforter adds a touch of casual pattern to the room without interrupting the peacefulness of the look.

This master bedroom was a "stay-away" rather than a getaway: Collectible stuffed toys, a patchwork quilt bedspread, and plain white walls left the space feeling uninspired. Frank creates a peaceful atmosphere using a palette of soft blues and greens paired with artistic shadowbox vignettes inspired by the sea.

Raise your hand if you've ever wished for a week, or even a day, away at a luxury spa. If you're among the many who would love just that kind of getaway, take a cue from this master bedroom transformation by Frank.

When one of the homeowners wished for "something that makes you feel like you went away on holiday," Frank uses glaze and clever accents to re-create the look of a seaside spa hotel.

First, however, the wife's collection of stuffed bears has to go to allow a more tranquil look to come in. Frank then establishes a quiet background with soft blue glaze to cover up white walls. Applying the glaze in small 3-foot squares allows enough time to drag a pick horizontally through the wet medium, creating a subtle strié pattern within understated blocks of blue. The process of covering the walls to the vaulted ceiling is time-consuming but worth the effort. For additional visual interest on the walls, Frank hand-paints vines throughout the space.

Turning his focus to the bed, Frank creates a headboard using three custom-built shadowbox rectangles with acrylic fronts and

▶before

▶Pennsylvania: Hillcrest Drive

The husband in this household makes it clear that he would really like to see his wife's collectible teddy bears leave their love nest—a wise choice because she is hoping that Frank will create "something like a spa hotel," and "something luxurious." She also says she would like a headboard and some nice drapes. The white walls and patchwork quilt can go.

▶Frank opted for a trio of rectangular shadowboxes to form this headboard, but you can do more or fewer. You could also make the shadowboxes in squares and hang them in a grid. Shadowboxes such as these can be filled with a wide variety of objects to establish your desired theme.

▶ Frank decided to save time in this episode by eliminating most sewing chores, so the blue sheers are purchased. This pillow was stitched, but you can create a similar look without sewing; use iron-on fusible hem table to join the seams and hot-glue decorative cord in place.

▲ MDF shadowboxes feature clear acrylic fronts and backs, allowing Frank and the neighbors to create small ocean-theme vignettes of sand, shells, and twigs. If you don't have time to build this shadowbox headboard, use stencils or stamps to paint a faux headboard.

▼ On each side of the bed, a side table with a seahorse base offers a whimsical touch. To make your own side table with a shapely base, create a pattern to outline onto plywood or MDF. Then cut out the design with a jigsaw. Spray paint your creation for a fast finish.

time crunch

▶ bed linens

Plain cotton sheets and comforters take on dynamic personality when you embellish them using these strategies:

▶ **IRON-ON TAPE** Secure ribbon and fabric appliqués to sheets and pillowcases using iron-on hem tape or fusible webbing.

▶ **FABRIC PAINTS** Add color and designs by applying painted patterns freehand or by using stencils or stamps.

▶ **BUTTONS** Even a novice sewer can stitch on a row or two of colorful buttons.

backs within blue-painted frames. Leaving the tops of the boxes open allows them to pour in sand and seashells and place branches to create beautiful seaside theme vignettes. Custom-built side tables with bases in the shape of seahorses add a playful touch on each side of the bed, which is dressed in a refreshing blue and white plaid comforter and crisp white pillows.

Instead of priming and painting a bedroom dresser and cabinet, Frank embellishes the grooved doors with white paint that he rubs on and off for a soft pickled wood effect. Low custom-built shelves provide additional storage and display space on each side of the dresser. Breezy blue sheers—purchased ready-made to save time—finish the room with airy, luxurious style.

▲ Just for fun, shelves in the small cube cabinets flanking the dresser hold gravel and baskets of shells.

grommet kits

Grommets are small metal rings that you punch through fabric to create reinforced holes for hooks, cords, braiding, or other materials. Grommets are an affordable way to attach hooks or cords to drapery panels, awnings, shower curtains, or any type of fabric panel. Decorative versions come in a range of colors and shapes, from snowflakes to stars, and can be used to add a custom touch to table linens, cloth ribbons, window treatments, and throw pillows.

Kits include everything you need to punch the hole into the fabric and to attach the grommet (which reinforces the hole); kits also provide the grommets themselves. For fail-safe results, look for kits that include a quality hole punch and a grommet-setting tool. Grommet kits retail for less than $20 and are available at crafts and hardware stores. Here are some additional ideas for using grommets:

▶ **ADD A DECORATIVE BORDER** to a ready-made place mat by evenly spacing colorful round eyelets about an inch from the edge of the place mat and then braiding a pretty ribbon through the grommets.

▶ **TO REDUCE HEAT** transference in a sunroom, fashion full-length fabric panels from inexpensive canvas and install 1-inch metal grommets at the top of the panels. Attach the panels to the window frames using a single curtain rod and colorful lengths of ribbon that have been looped through each of the grommets and over the rod.

▲ Frank painted the vines on the walls by hand, teaching one of the neighbors how to load the brush with two shades of green—one shade on each side of the brush—then pressing down and twisting to create a pointed leaf with variegated color. Using stencils or stamps can yield a similar look in even less time.

▲ This cabinet located beside the entry to the dressing area received a pickled treatment on its doors to match the dresser. Another painted plant appears near the floor beside the cabinet.

what you need

LETTER PERFECT

Materials
Handwritten letter
Adhesive-back
 dimensional dots
 (available at crafts
 and art supply
 stores)
Special photo
Frame
Mats (available at
 party supply stores)

accelerated artwork

Make a personal style statement by creating your own artwork. If you have access to a color photocopier or a photocopy store, you have the technology to transform special belongings into one-of-a-kind artwork that will impress your guests with its originality.

Letter perfect

Somewhere in a drawer or box, you may have a keepsake letter—a note from a special friend, a family heirloom correspondence, or perhaps a letter you discovered in a flea market book or box. For this project, a love letter was photocopied in color and enlarged to serve as a mat for another photocopy: this one a vintage wedding photo. Adhesive-back dimensional dots elevate the photograph slightly above the surface of the letter. A flower sticker adds a final decorative touch before framing. Because the letter and photograph are photocopies, this project is ideal when you want to give the same gift to several people—such as a wedding memory for family members. Adapt this idea to other combinations, such as a birth certificate and baby photo.

In an afternoon

what you need

OBJECTS OF AFFECTION

Materials

Objects to be photocopied
Piece of decorative paper or fabric
3 large square frames
4 smaller square frames

Objects of affection

Take your collection of tiny objects out of hiding. Select several small treasured items and have enlarged photocopies made of each one. Create visual unity by laying a piece of fabric or art paper behind each object as it's being photocopied. Here, a blue linen shirt served as the backdrop for each object; black frames and white mats also help unify the grouping. For variety in this arrangement, four smaller photocopies are grouped to equal the individual size of the larger photocopies.

White wow
Existing white crown molding makes the colors in the room seem even more pronounced.

Dimensional plus
A three-dimensional border, created with joint compound and a stencil, lends textural interest near the ceiling.

Feather fun
Ordinary lampshades take on a glamorous air in minutes with the addition of feathery trim.

Step up
An existing ladder gives both people and pooches a leg up on the extra tall bed. Using a different fabric on every rung adds another fun touch to the room.

Graceful sides
Custom-made side tables feature a graceful arch and finials to mimic the details of the bed.

Grand introduction
A grand wood bed, which the homeowners recently purchased, sets the stage for saturated colors and plush fabrics.

Plush purple
A color that exudes richness, purple makes the velvety fabric seem even more luxurious.

DESIGNED BY CHRISTI

color companions

In this bedroom Christi employs a striking palette of teal and purple and a collection of enticingly soft velvety fabrics; the mood is lavish and rich. Crisp white accents make the colors pop, and unusual features such as a stenciled textured border and feathery lighting give the room an exotic feel.

▶Minnesota: Pleasure Creek Circle

Orange walls distinguished by alternating polyurethane stripes "do nothing to set off the huge, beautiful bed," Christi says. The newlywed homeowners love bold color, however, and would like Christi to be courageous with the makeover palette. They're also hoping for better lighting and a window treatment.

A substantial and elegant bed that the homeowners had recently purchased establishes a grand tone for this master bedroom. The owners didn't want anything done to the bed itself; however, everyone seemed ready to say goodbye to the two-tone orange stripes on the walls. Because alternating stripes were layered in shiny polyurethane, a coat of primer came first to allow fresh top coats to adhere.

Before applying the top coat color, however, Christi adds a different kind of border along the top of each wall. Joint compound applied over a stencil creates a three-dimensional design that introduces a band of texture around the room.

With the border in place, Christi says she wants to create some more "theatrical pow," so she selects a courageous, complementary palette of teal for the walls and velvety purple fabrics for the bed. Darker teal glaze brushed over the textured border makes the design more prominent. White paint for the crown molding and the ceiling provides a dramatic contrast with the dark hue.

When choosing the wall and bed linen hues, Christi drew on colors found in a length of sheer fabric that now gracefully swags around a rod at the window. Painting the bedside shelves white to match the crown molding and the ceiling makes the teal wall color appear even more intense.

▶ shady solutions

Feathers make the lampshades in this bedroom playfully romantic. Select from all kinds of embellishments to customize your own shades. Use either a hot-glue gun or fabric glue to make decorative additions stick. Here are a few ideas:

▶ **BUTTONS AND BEADS** These come in all colors, sizes, and shapes. Apply them randomly, in stripes or borders, or all over.

▶ **TRIM TERRIFIC** You'll be amazed at the variety of fringes, braids, cords, and beaded trims that are available. Use them to outline the top and bottom of the shade or apply trim to follow the ribs on the shade. Cover an entire shade with overlapping fringe trim for a 1920s look.

▶ **FABRIC FINESSE** Use spray adhesive to form-fit fabric to the shade. Allow lightweight fabrics to fall more loosely by using hot glue to adhere only the edges of the fabric to the back side of the shade along the top and bottom rims.

▶ **PAINT PERFECT** Stamp, stencil, or paint designs freehand, using latex or fabric paints.

◀ Wall shelves work as well as regular bedside tables. In this room, Christi designed bedside shelves with an arch and finials to complement the bed.

▲ A hot-glue gun makes it easy to apply decorative trim, such as these feathers, on a purchased shade.

From the Designers

▶ **CHRISTI PROCTOR**

Q When you reflect on *Trading Spaces* rooms where you accomplished the most, what time-management strategies do you credit for your success?

A Good lists and being able to cull out things that were of little impact to the room.

Q Is it better to focus on one aspect (for example, wall color) of your entire home or solely on one room at a time?

A I think it's best to focus on one room at a time. Spend a little more on one or two extra-meaningful items, such as a sofa or your entertainment center. The rest you can spend less on now and add to later. Build around one or two good-quality, solid pieces.

Q When you're shopping, what's the biggest time-waster? What do you do to avoid it?

A Not having a list. With no focus, it's amazing how many tangents I get off on and lose the main purpose of my shopping. Lists also keep me from having to backtrack the aisles in places like home centers.

Q Do you use any painting shortcuts you use that don't significantly affect the results?

A Always do your prep work. A little time to tape off saves a ton of time touching up.

◄ With no rod pocket or stitching required, this window treatment provides style in a snap. The long sheer panel loosely swags over a decorative rod.

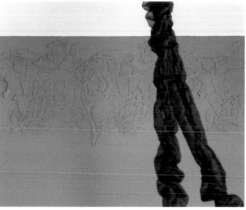

▲ Dark antiquing glaze dry-brushed onto the border subtly highlights the textured pattern added to the wall. Sheer fabric tubes cover a chain that suspends a lamp.

With an abundance of rich, dark hues now appearing in the room, better lighting is a must. Christi brings in a new five-armed chandelier that continues the elegant look of the room.

Adding more playful glamour, fixtures with feather-trimmed shades flank the bed. These lights are each suspended from chain wrapped in purple sheer fabric. Paired with the lights, custom-made shelves hang on the wall on each side of the bed to serve as nightstands. Finials and arched fasciae give the shelves a visual connection to the bed. Piles of pillows make the bed ultracomfortable, and two pillows embroidered with the names of the homeowners' pet Yorkies, Killer and Mango, finish the room with a smile.

Summing up the overall effect of her teal and wood-tone scheme, Christi proclaims, "It's sassy and sexy."

◄ Plush purples, animal prints, faux fur, and even a few feathers pile up at the head of the bed to make it more plush and inviting. (The names of the homeowners' dogs are embroidered on two pillows, reserving space for the lucky pooches.) Get this comfy look quickly by purchasing a host of similarly colored pillows and customizing them with beads, buttons, and decorative trim applied with a glue gun or whipstitched with needle and thread.

lightning-fast
lighting

In an afternoon

what you need

Materials
Lamp
Shade
Metallic leaf
Adhesive size for
  metallic leaf or
  spray adhesive
Clear spray sealer
Ribbon trim
Glass bead trim

Tools
Painter's tape
Scissors
Tweezers
Artist's brushes in
  wide and narrow
  sizes
Glue gun

Building a lamp from scratch is fun yet time-consuming. For lighting that's fast and stylish, begin with a thrift store or flea market lamp. The lamp featured here has an attractive green glass base; a wood, metal, or ceramic base would work equally well. Gather the necessary tools and materials—including a new lampshade— and follow these steps to dress up a lamp in metallic leaf and glass beads.

A.

B.

C.

1. **Clean the lamp base** to remove dust and oils. Dry thoroughly. Use painter's tape to cover portions of the lamp base that you don't plan to decorate with metallic leaf. Spray or brush on adhesive where you plan to apply metallic leaf. Cut individual sheets of the metallic leaf, keeping the tissue paper that comes with the leaf in place. Handle sheets carefully; they are extremely thin and fragile. Using tweezers, pick up the metallic leaf, keeping the sheet of tissue paper on top to protect the leaf. Position the tissue paper and leaf on the lamp base as desired (see Photo A).

2. **Remove the tissue paper** and use a soft artist's brush to smooth the leaf in place (see Photo B). To fill in small gaps between sheets or to repair spots where metallic leaf has accidentally peeled off, apply adhesive to

the gap; cut a small piece of leaf to cover it, and apply leaf as described in Step 1. Use a soft brush to brush away the unwanted metallic leaf. Let dry. Spray the applied leaf with clear sealer.

3. **To decorate the shade,** apply ribbon and glass bead trim with a hot-glue gun, pressing the ribbon and trim in place as you go (see Photo C). Begin applying the trim at the seam in the shade to avoid creating an extra visible seam. Finish applying trim by cutting the ribbon about $\frac{1}{2}$ inch longer than needed; fold the raw edge under and glue in place.

Treatment topper
A fabric-covered wood cornice gives the window treatment a finished, custom look while hiding an unattractive rod.

Balanced lighting
Lamps flank the sofa to create classic symmetry—a look that complements the geometric shapes in this living room.

Pillow talk
The striped fabric forms a square design on the pillows when it's cut into triangular pieces and sewn to intersect.

Banished beige
Formerly beige, this thrift store sofa wears a deep blue slipcover that coordinates with other blue fabrics in the room.

Table transformation
Glass insets dated this coffee table. Substituting hardboard for the glass and wrapping the new insets in leatherlike vinyl pulls the piece into the present—a quick and inexpensive solution.

block party

DESIGNED BY DOUG

Squares and stripes unite in this living room, which shapes up to be both casual and elegant. After choosing a window fabric with star-sprinkled stripes, Doug dubs the space "Purely Presidential." The room is an appealing, contemporary candidate sure to remain popular for years to come.

▶Minneapolis: 11th Avenue

Walls rag-rolled in beige combined with beige sofas and—you guessed it—beige pillows left this room feeling as dull as a rainy day. The homeowner spends all her time in this living room and says she is ready for warm color. She also feels the sofas are too large for the room and hopes Doug can produce soft seating that's smaller and more interesting.

Comfortable and inviting are the words that homeowners often use to describe how they wish their rooms would feel. The owner of this living room joins the ranks, adding that she's tired of the beige-on-beige look of the space where she spends a great deal of time. She asks Doug for a warmer palette—definitely something brighter than beige. She'd also love to see more-streamlined sofas and points out that she and her friends are always stubbing their toes on the entertainment center, which sits at an angle in a corner between two passageways into adjoining rooms.

Doug finds a bright beginning for the space in the form of fabric sporting bold yellow and crisp white stripes spiced with narrow blue star-studded stripes. With this grand fabric in hand, he decides to label the room "Purely Presidential."

Doug starts the transformation by covering up the rag-rolled beige walls with a coat of white. Then he follows up with a clever faux paint treatment that gives the walls the look of ancient parchment paper. (The mix of ivory and tan paint colors creates a softer version of the yellow found in the fabric.) Doug's paint treatment produces overlapping rectangles of color; along with the fabric stripes and the squares of color on the rug, the pattern on the wall establishes a stylish geometric element.

▲Though the pillows in this room are sewn, iron-on fusible webbing can join fabric pieces for the same effect.

▶As a playful turn, the seat cushion on the chair features the same striped fabric that appears on the pillows, but the stripes are joined to form triangles rather than the squares.

◀If you have little time to tend houseplants, consider tasteful silk versions. Doug selected a pair of sculptural topiaries that introduce soft yet substantial flashes of green into the room.

◄ ◄ The new entertainment center nestles into a corner, providing a clearer traffic pattern through the room and gobbling up much less floor space.

◄ Glass insets were removed from the coffee table, and hardboard panels wrapped in black faux leather were installed—an easy style update that requires little time to complete.

time crunch

► coffee tables

Dressing up an existing coffee table with fabric or paint is only one fast fix-up idea. Here are some other ways to get a trendy table in minutes:

► **DOOR PRIZE** Salvage yards, flea markets, and antiques stores are all good sources for vintage doors at reasonable prices. Tote one home and use it as a coffee table top mounted on stacks of hardcover books for support. Or use decorative concrete patio wall blocks as legs.

► **PLAYTIME** While browsing flea markets and antiques shops, watch for out-of-service items such as old toy wagons or small carts that could stand in as a playfully rustic coffee table. If you wish, top the wagon or cart with glass.

► **WHEEL STYLE** Reproduction advertising signs fashioned from metal make good tabletops. Add casters to get this coffee table idea rolling. For a more elegant look, add purchased turned legs to the bottom of a framed vintage print.

► **GLASS CLASS** Introduce glamour with an all-glass coffee table. Start with a glass tabletop cut to the desired size. (For safety have the glass cutter round the corners.) Stack up a base of glass blocks (such as those used as window inserts) and add a light in the center of the base. Thread the cord underneath one of the blocks. Position the glass tabletop on top of the glass-block base.

With a brighter, more contemporary look under way, the old sofas seemed too bulky and bland for the room. Doug offers three thrift store sofas for the neighbors to choose from, pointing out that the one with fewer curves will look better and be much faster to slipcover. They all agree, and a navy blue slipcover—which offers neutral compatibility similar to denim—makes the old sofa a fashion plus for the space.

Pillows made from the same fabric as the window treatments make the streamlined sofa more comfortable; an old coffee table—remade with leather-look insets—adds style and practicality.

Rather than keep the old toe-smashing entertainment center, Doug specifies a custom-built corner unit that fits more neatly into the same location. He starts by covering up the MDF surfaces with bold navy blue, then tones down the color with a mixture of black paint, glaze, and water lightly applied with a brush.

For some easy-care finishing flair, Doug brings in artificial topiaries that he says are reminiscent of the Washington Monument—the ideal accessory for a room that's "Purely Presidential."

plant a memory

what you need

In a few hours

Materials
Assorted terra-cotta
  pots
Assorted small objects
  or mementos
Pre-mixed ceramic tile
  adhesive and grout,
  sanded white
Spray polyurethane

Tools
Putty knife
Rubber gloves

A.

If you come back from vacation toting loads of souvenirs such as postcards, seashells, key rings, souvenir spoons, and refrigerator magnets, put them to use. Put your great memories on display by using them to decorate containers for outdoor or indoor plants.

1. **Wipe pot surface** to remove dust. Wear rubber gloves and spread adhesive grout on the surface, working in small patches (see Photo A).

2. **Press shells, rocks,** or other found objects or souvenirs into adhesive to secure to the pot. Cover base up to the rim of the pot. Let adhesive dry according to container directions.

3. **Protect small objects,** especially paper postcards, by sealing the entire surface with polyurethane spray. Let dry. Apply a second coat of sealer, if desired.

4. **Fill pots** with plants and flowers. Display indoors or out.

the decorating pantry ▶

markers

Whether you need to label a box or decorate a window or wall, you'll find a marking pen available for the job. Explore the variety of markers at crafts, art, discount, and office supply stores. Plan to keep at least three different kinds in your decorating pantry:

▶ **FELT-TIP MARKERS** Available with either washable or permanent inks, felt-tip markers can be used to decorate anything from paper decorations to vinyl roller shades. Felt-tip markers cannot be used on finished drywall, however, because the ink tends to bleed—even through multiple coats of paint.

▶ **PAINT MARKERS** Applying pressure to the valve tip of these markers releases the flow of the paint. Available with metallic or oil-base paint in a variety of colors, the markers are ideal for use on drywall, fabrics, plaster, wood, and most plastics.

▶ **GLASS MARKERS** These are specially designed paint markers that can be used to mark glass or mirrors. The paint dries quickly, stays on in the rain, and is easy to remove with a wet cloth. With a glass marker, you can draw pumpkins or snowflakes on the front window of your home or messages of encouragement on your children's bathroom mirror.

Tall-order draperies

New curtain panels extend from ceiling to floor for a grand appearance. The white fabric blends with the walls to keep the look uninterrupted.

Dare to pair

Create mini themes throughout the room with artwork you love. This dynamic duo adds visual punch to the shelves on page 112.

Seating savvy

The existing earth-tone love seats and a chair were keepers for the makeover. The solid-brown fabric is in good condition and suits the quiet, contemporary look.

DESIGNED BY HILDI

art centered

As she helps a couple pare down their belongings, Hildi demonstrates how less has greater impact than more. Neutral tones and a wood parquet floor establish an elegant backdrop for showing off dramatic original artwork.

A few good pieces
Originally the extensive artwork collection climbed to the peak of the vaulted ceiling. Paring down to a few good pieces leaves some blank space—a place for the eye to rest—and lets the artwork on display stand out.

Tactile walls
Joint compound applied to the walls and feathered with a trowel introduces subtle, eye-pleasing texture to the room. A fresh coat of white paint provides a clean start.

Skirt the issue
A white fabric slipcover stylishly tops the television stand to make it less noticeable—a quick fix for any unsightly furnishing.

Warm wood tone
Wood parquet floor tiles balance the white walls with warm color and subtle tone-on-tone pattern.

Woven base
A natural berber area rug provides a visual anchor for furnishings and offers soft texture underfoot.

before

▶ Florida: Night Owl Lane

The avid art collectors who live here admit that their living room looks overcrowded with so many pieces filling the walls. Blue-green carpeting and arched-door cabinets clash with the chic contemporary feel of the framed art.

f you're a collector you can probably relate to the affection the owners of this living room feel for their extensive collection of artwork and other items. Many of the paintings were done by the father of one of the homeowners, making those pieces all the more beloved. In fact, at the beginning of the episode, one of the homeowners admits, "We don't have the guts ourselves to take some things out and focus on a few things in the room, so we are counting on some design help to do that for us." Hildi undertakes the challenge and pulls everything out of the room—including a dated pair of cabinets—to begin with a clean slate.

Forest green carpeting leaves the room too, with Hildi breathing a sigh of relief that it isn't glued down. Wood parquet tiles replace the carpeting, introducing classic elegance and warmth. "I'm hoping [the wood parquet tiles] will make the room look larger, cleaner, and crisper," Hildi says.

Rather than leave the walls plain, she adds more low-key character with a thick layer of joint compound that's feathered with a trowel to create texture. Though the texture gives visual dimension to the room, it won't call attention away from the artwork.

◄ ◄ A pair of cabinets once occupied this spot. Adding the partition wall on the right formed a niche to accommodate a trio of 2½-foot deep shelves. Leaning the artwork against the wall, rather than hanging it, saves time and yields a casual, contemporary look. This approach also makes it easy for the homeowners to bring other pieces out of storage and quickly rotate the exhibit.

▲ Bold colors unify these two paintings, which stand out against the subtly textured walls. The transition between rough and smooth wall surfaces lends dimension and interest without overpowering the arrangement.

time crunch

► painted furniture

Hildi visited a thrift store and found "a mountain" of coffee tables and end tables free for the taking, she says. She used primer and paint to give the pieces she selected an updated look. Consider these timesavers the next time you plan to paint furniture.

► **REUSE** When you dislike the look of a room, it's tempting to eliminate all the pieces and start over with new ones. Instead of buying unfinished wood furniture at discount stores, save yourself the assembly time (and the cost) by reusing and painting wood pieces that you already own. You'll be amazed at how great an old table, chair, or cabinet looks with a new coat of paint.

► **SAND** Take the time to sand. Sanding makes surfaces smooth and touchable; it also makes the paint adhere better. Wipe the surface with a tack cloth to remove sanding residue.

► **PRIME** It's information worth repeating: Always apply primer because, without this barrier, the old finish or wood resins may seep through the painted finish. When that happens you lose time because you have to paint again.

► **SPRAY** Instead of paintbrushes and rollers, consider using spray paint. (Spray primer is also available.) To ensure a smooth, drip-free finish, shake the can well and hold the can above the surface at a distance recommended by the manufacturer. Point the nozzle off the surface of the furniture, depress the button, and then sweep the spray onto the surface, applying a very light layer of paint to avoid drips. Move your arm smoothly back and forth to keep the application even. Let the piece dry for the recommended amount of time before applying additional thin layers.

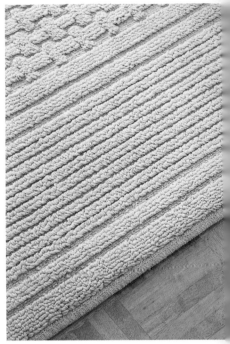

▲ Glue-down application was the fast, practical method for installing these wood parquet tiles. At 98 cents per square foot, the tiles demanded about 30 percent of the budget, according to Hildi.

▶ Hildi sorted through a huge number of wonderful paintings before deciding on this desert-hues grouping. The paintings complement one another and support the earth-tone furnishings too.

time crunch

▶ window treatments

Here are some in-a-flash strategies for creating great-looking window treatments:

▶ **FOLD 'EM** Snap a tension rod into the window frame and drape fabric—such as a tablecloth or piece of lace—over the rod.

▶ **TACK 'EM** Stretch fabric across the top of the window and use decorative nailheads or tacks to secure the fabric in place.

▶ **STICK 'EM** Use adhesive-backed hook-and-loop tape to fix fabric to the window frame.

▶ **CLIP 'EM** Snap clip-on rings onto curtain panels, vintage linens, or old tablecloths (folded in half to fit, if necessary) to hang fabric in mere minutes.

▶ **THREAD 'EM** Snap a tension rod into the window frame and thread a prefabricated panel onto the rod.

▶ **FUSE 'EM** Hem fabric panels with iron-on hem tape. Use the same tape to create a rod pocket at the top of the panel. Slide the pocket over a tension rod and mount it in the window frame.

▶ **TIE 'EM** Install grommets across the top of a curtain panel or tablecloth (or cut slits if you're really pressed for time). Thread lengths of ribbon, cording, or rope through the grommets or slits and tie the curtain panel to a rod.

◀ The berber rug and parquet flooring provide visual interest without stealing attention from the artwork.

To make up for the absence of the cabinets, Hildi adds a shallow partition perpendicular to the wall where the cabinets once stood, forming a display niche. Three shelves built into the niche allow the owners to show off well-chosen pieces of artwork as well as books and figurines.

Though much of this room makeover involves deleting, Hildi does keep the homeowners' original sofas and chair. The plain brown fabric and uncomplicated lines make these pieces smart companions for the contemporary art gallery theme. "No pillows," Hildi says. "Everything is just going to be very simple." She keeps her promise by defining the seating area with an understated berber rug and plain, off-white draperies at the patio door.

"The changes that we made were grand," Hildi says, summing up. "The wall, the texture, the floor obviously took up the highest part of the budget. But like I say, just focus on one or two things."

what you need

Materials
Leather hides, about 25 square feet in two colors—enough to make a 4×6-foot rug

Leather lacing, about 10 yards

Tools
Grommet kit with hole-punch tool

Hammer

Scissors

Note: To find leather hides, check online sources as well as upholstery goods outlets in your area. Leather lacing is available in crafts stores.

luxurious leather rug

You've probably noticed that leather is in. On sofas and headboards, in decorative accessories, and even as floor tiles, this supple, sexy material is appearing in almost every room in the house. This laced rug features two shades of leather. Easy to assemble in an afternoon, it brings a rich touch to an entryway, family room, or bedroom.

A.

B.

1. **Using sharp scissors,** cut 2×2-foot squares from two shades of leather. Cut the inside edges of each square straight so they will fit evenly against each other; use existing raw edges of the hide for outside edges. If outside edges are too uneven, trim them in soft curves for a natural look. The finished leather rug shown here measures about 4×6 feet and features six leather squares—three of each shade.

2. **Mark grommet holes** every 2 inches along the inside edges, about 1 inch from the edge (see Photo A). Note that middle squares have grommets on three sides; corner squares have grommets on two sides. Punch holes with the tool provided in the kit, following package directions. Position the halves of the grommet ring on each side of the hole; use tool and hammer to join the grommet pieces as directed.

3. **Join the leather squares** by weaving leather lacing through the grommets in shoelace fashion (see Photo B). Tie the leather lacing at the ends.

the decorating pantry

adhesives

Keep yourself out of many sticky situations by keeping these varieties of adhesives on hand:

▶ **ALL-PURPOSE LIQUID GLUE** In addition to bonding papers, woods, and pottery, this white adhesive dries clear and can be used for decoupaging (mix equal parts of glue and water), repairing wallcoverings, and adding lightweight embellishments to all sorts of accessories, from lampshades to picture frames.

▶ **PHOTO-SAFE GLUE** This specially formulated acid-free glue is ideal for use in memory albums and with keepsakes of all kinds. It dries clear without wrinkling, curling, or yellowing and is available in spray, stick, and liquid form.

▶ **SUPERGLUE** Whether you want to restore the legs of small tables or reassemble a broken vase or statue, this fast-bonding glue will do the job. It bonds almost any combination of surfaces together— including fingers. (If you find your fingers stuck together with superglue, use acetone nail polish remover to break down the glue, or soak your fingers in hot, soapy water until the bond softens. Make sure no one else sees you because you will never hear the end of it.)

▶ **HOT GLUE** A quality glue gun and a package of glue sticks cost less than $15. The time these products can save you is well worth the investment. Hot glue adheres adornments to nearly everything the *Trading Spaces* crew designs, from vases to picture frames.

▶ **GLUE STICKS** Keep an assortment of fat and skinny glue sticks in your decorating pantry for adhering paper projects and other lightweight materials. Because your hands never have to touch the glue, this is a great product for kids. (Some sticks even produce glue that turns fun colors once it dries.) Glue sticks that are safe for photos are also available. For a nature-inspired kids' project, use glue sticks to adhere found leaves (or construction paper leaves) around construction paper place mats.

▶ **SPRAY ADHESIVE** Whenever you use spray adhesive, work outdoors or in a well-ventilated area. This product is especially good for mounting artwork on a mat or other surface, such as wood. Or apply spray adhesive on a surface that you plan to wrap in fabric (such as a foam cushion) because the adhesive lets the fabric remain flexible and provides a tacky surface that prevents sagging. To make a table runner in minutes, secure layers of fabric (that you don't plan to wash) using spray adhesive.

Easy green
Green with yellow undertones is reminiscent of a freshly unfurled leaf. The wall color makes the room feel sunny, even on a cloudy day.

windows on nature

Prints charming
Framed by salvaged window sashes, the botanical prints provide an imaginary view on each side of the existing window. The prints were enlarged at a copy center.

Growing style
Houseplants play up the nature theme and make the setting more lively.

DESIGNED BY GENEVIEVE

In this living room designed by Gen, substantial oak woodwork and wood flooring suggested the botanical nature theme. Leaf green walls, crisp white accents, and large-scale botanical prints breathe a fresh-as-spring attitude into a vintage house.

Comfort plus
An armload of pillows is one of the surest ways to make a room more inviting. This cluster of pillows also complements the invigorating color scheme of the room.

Pane relief

Salvage yards are a great source for bargain window sashes, such as these. Flanking the existing windows with additional window frames echoes the look of an adjoining window-wrapped office, page 120.

Under cover

An old white ottoman introduces the all-important touch of black with a new slipcover. White braid accents at cushion level—attached in minutes—connect the piece with the existing sofa.

Toasty tootsies

Although wood floors are gorgeous, they can bo cold in winter. This area rug ensures warmth underfoot while defining the seating area.

► Fabric panels can be drawn closed for privacy in the living room office alcove. Panels such as these install quickly, thanks to clip-on rings that slip onto the decorative rod.

before

ntriguing nooks and wonderful woodwork are often part of the allure of old houses, and this home offers both. Gen accepts the assignment to redo the living room, which features broad oak baseboards, warm plank floors, and a window-wrapped alcove. Although everyone concerned appreciates the great character of the space, Gen and the homeowner agree that the dark brown on the walls has to go.

Armed with a batch of window sash that she found at an architectural salvage yard (only $5 for the bunch), Gen carries the look of the sunny alcove into the living room. "The window sashes are part of the inspiration of the room," she says. "We'll make a wall of windows in the living room to match the [alcove]."

►**Minneapolis: 11th Ave.**

"Great house, wrong color," Gen says when she sees this living room in an older home. The woodwork is a terrific bonus, as is a window-wrapped alcove to the right of the sofa. Gen and the homeowner want to banish the brown wall color. Wisely, they decide to maintain and enhance the classic character of the room.

▼ Lush fringe, such as this black bullion, can be added to an existing sofa or ottoman as a fresh detail. Use hot glue to secure fringe or cording in place.

▶ soup up a sofa

Gen quickly dressed up the homeowner's existing white sofa by adding black fringe around the bottom. Upholstered pieces transform in a flash with these strategies:

▶ **SLIP OVER** Check catalogs and online sources for stylish, great-fitting ready-made slipcovers that give chairs, sofas, and ottomans a whole new look in an instant. Slipcovers are a great way to change color palettes and fabrics with the seasons.

▶ **STAMP ON** To add color and pattern to a solid-color sofa (or slipcover), stencil or stamp designs on the fabric. Check crafts stores for paints that wear well on fabrics.

▶ **LOOK DOWN** Give an old sofa new attitude by replacing existing legs with purchased wood legs in a different style. Most home centers stock a variety of turned legs and bun feet to suit your style. Or use paint to perk up existing wood feet on a sofa. Consider creating a more contemporary look by replacing legs with casters.

First, however, she uses two shades of spring green to brighten the walls, choosing the darker of the two greens for the main living room and a slightly lighter shade for the alcove.

Four crisp white window sashes are hung on adjacent walls to augment the existing window in the sitting area of the living room. Screen covers the openings in two of the vintage window frames, and botanical prints—photocopied from a used book that Gen's mother found for $10—fill the remaining two frames.

"It really gives the back wall the focal point that the room was definitely missing," Gen says of the arrangement.

◀ This captivating tabletop arrangement rests on a salvaged window sash placed on the ottoman. Stones placed in an attractive shallow bowl and interspersed with tea light candles create an easy and elegant accent.

▲ Transform the look of a lamp in a flash with purchased shades. These black fabric-covered shades infuse the room with elegance for little investment in time or money.

▶ The top two compartments of this cabinet were constructed to match the dimensions of another salvaged window sash with glass intact. The sash now functions as the cabinet door.

metallic finishes

Metallic paints and leafing kits let you add a shiny metal finish to any smooth, sealed surface, including fabric, glass, metal, plaster, wood, and most plastics.

▶ **LATEX-BASE METALLIC PAINTS** are available at crafts stores for about $1 per ounce. They're perfect for faux finishing, sponge painting, and adding metallic accents to decorative accessories such as candleholders, lamps, vases, and frames. Metallic paint can also highlight carving on a dresser or other furniture. Use a clean rag to dab paint onto the carving, then dab some of the paint off with a clean rag.

▶ **METALLIC LEAFING KITS** are also available at crafts stores. They contain microthin sheets of metal similar to aluminum foil, a special adhesive size to make the sheets stick to the desired surface, and a soft brush to smooth the metal sheeting onto the surface. Although more expensive and more difficult to use than metallic paints, metallic leaf creates a finish that looks more like metal, with eye-pleasing depth and shine. Choose this material if you want to make a plaster sconce or statue appear cast from metal, for example. Or use metallic leaf to add glamour to a wood frame or lamp base. Metallic leafing comes in a variety of affordable compositions, including gold, silver, copper, and zinc. To cover a surface with one of these composition metal sheets, plan to spend about $1.75 per square foot of coverage (small kits provide enough leafing for about 6 square feet and retail for about $10). Porous surfaces (such as plaster or raw wood) need to be sealed with gesso or a similar sealer prior to application of the adhesive. Nonporous surfaces such as glass and hard plastic don't require sealing. Coating the top of the applied leafing sheets with additional coats of sealer prevents the metals from oxidizing, tarnishing, or flaking. For a vintage look, paint a base coat of color onto the surface and let dry before applying the adhesive size. The color can then peek through any gaps in the metallic leaf, creating an appealing visual effect much like a weathered finish on furniture.

The homeowner's sofa and ottoman earn makeovers too: Black fringe jazzes up the white sofa, and a black slipcover with white trim transforms the old ottoman. One more window sash goes to good use in the sitting area: The old window acts as a charming door for an entertainment cabinet custom-made by Amy Wynn.

Gen finishes the makeover by putting the alcove to work as an office space. She brings in an old desk that she discovered in the basement and adds fabric curtain panels (which match new window treatments in the main living room). The panels can be closed for office privacy.

▲ Save time on creating artwork by having a copy center make it for you. Gen had pages from an old book enlarged for about $20. Decoupage glue, swiped onto the window glass in minutes, holds the photocopies in place.

From the Designers

▶ GENEVIEVE GORDER

Q In addition to the home furnishings and accessories departments at discount stores, what other departments are worth visiting for cool decorating materials and ideas?

A I like the hardware aisles. Look at the bare essentials of construction—the nuts and bolts of it all—and your resourceful inner designer should awaken. It seems the most simple and ordinary of things always become the most extraordinary when used in a creatively different way than they were intended.

I also like to go to the aisle where I would find clothing that I might wear. Fashion is one facet of design that has the highest, most frequent rate of change. It's so transitional—look to this form of design for inspiration in your home. Tailored lines in shirts and dresses always make their way down to the stylings in pillows, curtains—and even color palettes.

Q Is it a better investment of time and money to focus on one aspect (for example, wall color) of your entire home or to focus solely on one room at a time?

A You should have an idea of what you want your home to feel like before you begin. Ask yourself where you feel most comfortable in life outside of your home. Is it at somebody else's home? A restaurant? A travel destination? A different time in your life? A spa? With a particular person?

Once you pinpoint this, create a list of keywords about this environment as it pertains to all of your senses. What colors did you see? How did it smell? And so on.

When you have your list, clarity will soon follow. When you have a general vibe for what you want your entire house to embrace, work with that idea in the back of your head as you attack it room by room. While each room can have its own personality, it is part of a larger whole, a family of sorts. Make sure there are connections with lighting and color so that the house will flow as you pass through.

Laid-back laminates

For a casual party, go with paper lanterns, place mats, and napkins. Nix the paper plates and set out white china instead.

Have place mats laminated at a quick-print shop that offers laminating services. Use the large paper cutter at the shop to trim the place mats, leaving a ½-inch clear edge around each mat.

● ● ● ● ● ● ● ● ● ● ● ● **In an hour**

what you need

LAID-BACK LAMINATES

Materials

Colorful paper place mats (available at party supply stores)

top-notch tabletop ideas

Guests are coming, and you want the table to look special without spending hours pulling it all together. Whether you're dining formally or casually, a great tabletop begins with one set of plain-white dishware. Then use these ideas to create table accessories that enhance the setting, whether it's black-tie or laid-back and colorful.

A quick ring

Hand-print guests' names on card stock or use a computer to do the job. Take printed card stock to a quick-print shop to have 2×3½-inch individual cards cut and laminated; ask the shop to leave a ⅛-inch clear edge around each card.

Slip curtain rings onto napkins. Clip on place cards.

Chalk one up

Instead of place cards, set the table with handmade chalkboards marked with guests' names. Follow these steps to make the mats:

Cut the hardboard into six 13×19-inch rectangles, using a circular saw or table saw. Or save time by having the home center cut the rectangles for you.

Paint the rectangles on one side with chalkboard paint; let dry. Paint the opposite side of each piece, touch up edges, and let dry.

Use chalk to write names or messages on each place mat.

To finish, combine frosted and clear glasses with earthy accessories, such as a wooden bowl centerpiece filled with coconuts. Cut a few coconuts in half, clear out the coconut, and fill the shells with sugar lumps, single-serve creamers, candy, nuts, or trail mix.

southwestern sizzle

String zing
Diamond-shape yarn art suits the Southwestern theme and repeats colors launched by the blanket-topped coffee table.

Nature talk
No Southwestern space is complete without a cactus. This one stands in a terra-cotta-colored pot.

Shelf expression
A pair of horizontal cabinets introduces striking architecture reminiscent of a rustic timber-built structure. Although the posts appear to run straight through the interior of the shelves, the 4×4s inside the cabinets are actually separate from the support posts.

Blanket decision
An old coffee table takes on a festive attitude when topped with a Mexican-style blanket wrapped around layers of soft batting.

Border beauty

Embossed wallpaper brings new dimension to the top of the wall. Painting the border orange and bronze makes it resemble rusty tin ceiling tiles.

Sand and sky

Colors borrowed from the Southwest wash the walls in a blend of desert hues.

Slim seating

Director's chairs provide additional stylish seating and another opportunity to introduce dashes of black into the room.

Urn this

Standing in as a one-of-a-kind occasional table is a pottery urn topped with a glass round— a look that can be duplicated in minutes.

Southwestern style comes to Kentucky when Edward layers this once white-walled living room in desert hues of blue-green turquoise, adobe orange, sunset red, and sunny yellow. Rustic horizontal cabinets supported by substantial posts answer the call for better organization without interrupting the theme. Dashes of black finish the clean yet playful space, which Edward aptly dubs "Mexican Modern."

►Louisville: Lantern Light Pkwy.

Filled with sofas, cabinets, occasional tables, and even a dining table and chairs, this living room has a whole lot going on. Little wonder, then, that the homeowners want Edward to create some order out of the chaos. "Our house is kind of a hodgepodge," one homeowner admits. They're also wishing for a brighter look and an entertainment center.

◄ If you don't have time or skill to sew your own Southwestern valance and curtain panels, consider this alternative: Purchase a table runner or tablecloth in the desired pattern and color. Pair up the runner or tablecloth with complementary purchased curtain panels. Clip the runner to the tops of the panels with clip-on curtain rings (or fold the tablecloth in half and clip to rings). Then slide the rings onto a rod.

▼ Top an urn or large vase with a glass round to create a side table in an instant. If the inside of the urn isn't as attractive as this one, try the approach shown on page 36.

f you're stalled out on a style for your room, draw on scenes from a favorite vacation spot or a place you'd like to visit. In this family room by Edward, the homeowners gained a Southwestern-style getaway without ever leaving town.

Mexican-striped blanket fabric offered the inspiration for all the colors in the room—a welcome change for a family who said they were tired of the lackluster look of their room.

Transforming the white walls with swirls of color, Edward's team rolled on patches of blue-green and blended in spots of yellow with a sponge. Orange dabbed intermittently with a nubby car-washing mitt and softened with a sponge lends a pleasing glow to the color blend.

The family knew that their room was a hodgepodge of furniture and that it lacked organization; Edward knew how to fix it: He

◄ Because the paint colors are randomly applied, a faux paint treatment such as the one Edward used here can be created in an afternoon. Enlist helpers to make the job go quickly and smoothly.

◀ Edward fashioned this soft coffee table in a jiffy, wrapping a wood tabletop with batting and fabric and then stapling the fabric edges underneath the tabletop. A strip of nailhead trim gives the piece a final rustic flourish.

honed down their belongings, keeping the oversize sectional and positioning it at an angle across the center of the room. End tables, a coffee table, and a desk discovered in the basement received primer and coats of black paint to join the new look. Covering the coffee table with batting and the blanket fabric allows this piece to double as a colorful ottoman.

A valance on the new curtain panels uses the same blanket fabric and pulls more color to the walls, where Edward caps off the faux paint treatment with an embossed border. Orange and bronze paint give the border the look of rusty tin ceiling tiles.

Almost every family room features a television and all the paraphernalia that goes with it; deciding how to store all these things can be a challenge. While a traditional armoire would have worked for the space, Edward opted for an alternative that continues the Southwestern theme. Long black and red horizontal cabinets, supported by posts that appear to run through the shelves, hang

From the Designers

▶ EDWARD WALKER

Q What time-management strategies do you credit for your successful room makeovers on the show?

A I think the biggest thing is having a clear plan and sticking to it. I did a kitchen where we redid the floor, painted the walls and ceiling, painted the appliances, put glass in the cabinet doors, and hung new window treatments and a chandelier. I had a concrete plan of what I was going to do and then figured out what I was going to do first. In this redo, we painted the ceiling first so no paint would get on the new floor. The appliances had to go outside to put the floor in, so while the appliances were outside, I spray-painted the stove and refrigerator.

Q Do you have any painting shortcuts?

A When painting a dark color, prime the walls with a tinted primer. My dining room is burgundy, so I used a dark gray primer, and then the burgundy top coat covered better. They make primers that can be tinted, but sometimes primers can't be tinted really dark, so choose a gray or purple and go as dark as you can go in tinting the primer. Then apply the final wall color.

Q What sort of items would you stock in your decorating pantry?

A In terms of tools, I definitely would have an electric staple gun with staples, a tack hammer, and probably a hot-glue gun. Me, I always have a sewing machine available somewhere.

Then accessorywise, I always have uplights with the bulbs that go with them and pillar candles with the glasses they can go in or something that they sit on so they won't go all over the table. I would probably include some type of cording too.

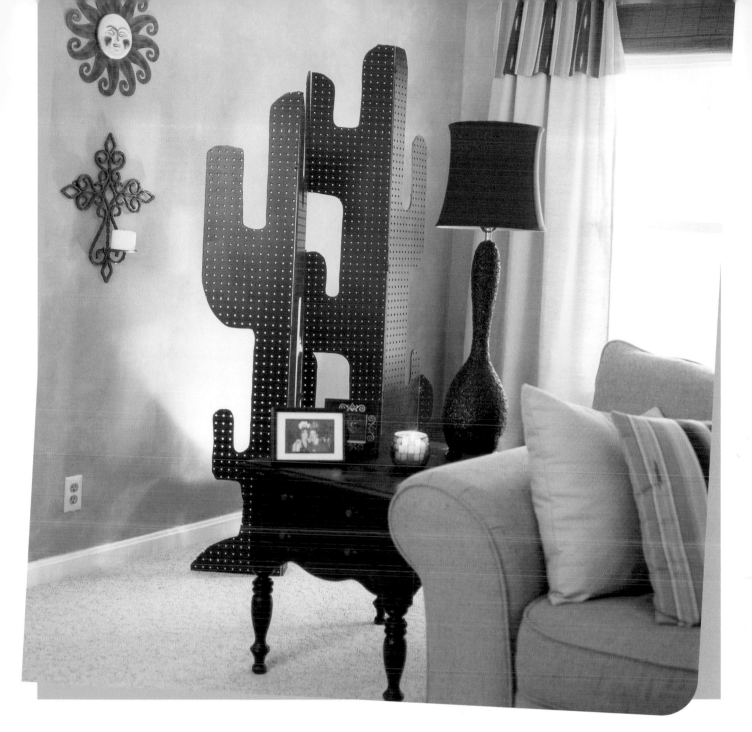

on adjacent walls at different heights. Diamond-shape medallions provide more color in a motif that fits the theme.

As a final clever touch, a folding pegboard screen cut into cactus shapes brings dimension to another corner of the room.

Eyeing the finished results, Edward sums up the look: "I think in the back of my mind I've been saying 'Mexican Modern.'"

The label definitely fits the clean, colorful results, and the look suits the homeowners, who now have a fun getaway right in their own home.

▲ A folding screen such as this cactus design requires only a few hours to make. Draw the desired shapes onto pegboard or ¼-inch-thick plywood. (Or use an opaque projector to cast the image you want onto sheet goods propped against a wall; trace the outline of the image with a pencil or marker.) Use the manufactured long edges of the sheet goods to form the straight side of each panel. Cut out the panels with a jigsaw; prime and paint. After the panels dry, join them with hinges.

in-a-jiffy knobs and pulls

··········· **In an hour or less**

what you need

U-BOLT HANDLE
Materials
One ⁵⁄₁₆×1⅜-inch U-bolt
  (or select a bolt that's
  the appropriate size
  for the thickness of the
  door or drawer front)
Four ⁵⁄₁₆-inch nuts (two
  nuts typically come
  with the U-bolt)

CARRIAGE-BOLT PULL
Materials
One ½×3-inch
  carriage bolt
Two ½-inch 13-square
  nuts

TURNBUCKLE HANDLE
Materials
One ³⁄₁₆×5½-inch
  turnbuckle
Two ¼-inch 20×3-inch
  flat-slotted machine
  screws
Six ¼-inch nuts

HITCH PULL
Materials
One 1⅞×¾×1½-inch
  chrome trailer-hitch
  ball (the ball comes
  with an appropriately
  sized nut)

One of the fastest ways to perk up old bathroom or kitchen cabinets, dressers, or other furniture, is to trade the old knobs and pulls for new ones. While you can choose from an abundance of new manufactured styles, you can create a hip, industrial look by quickly assembling your own knobs and pulls. You'll find the needed supplies readily available in the hardware aisle of a home center or hardware store.

1. **U-bolt handle** Drill two holes in the drawer or door front to accommodate the U-bolt.

Screw two nuts onto the U-bolt legs. Next slide on the flat plate that comes with the U-bolt. Place the legs of the U-bolt through the holes. (The flat plate will be on the outside of the drawer or door front.)

Screw the remaining two nuts onto the U-bolt legs on the back of the drawer or door (see Photo A). Tighten the four nuts until the U-bolt is evenly positioned.

2. **Carriage-bolt pull** Drill one ½-inch hole in the drawer or door front to accommodate the carriage bolt.

Screw one square nut onto the carriage bolt with the beveled edge facing the bolt head (see Photo B). Place the carriage bolt through the drilled hole.

Screw the second square nut onto the carriage bolt on the back of the drawer or door front with the beveled edge facing away from the back of the drawer or door front.

Tighten the two square nuts until the carriage bolt is held evenly in place.

3. **Turnbuckle handle** Drill two holes in the drawer or door front to accommodate the spacing of the two pre-drilled holes in the ends of the turnbuckle.

Tighten the two eyebolts on the turnbuckle until they are protruding equally from the ends of the turnbuckle.

Slide the two machine screws into the turnbuckle eyebolts and twist two nuts onto the screws, tightening the screw heads against the turnbuckle (see Photo C). (This forms the handle.)

Twist two more nuts onto the machine screws and insert the newly constructed handle in the drilled holes.

Screw the last two nuts onto the ends of the screws protruding through the back of the drawer or door front.

Tighten the four nuts on either side of the drawer or door front until the handle is held evenly in place.

4. **Hitch pull** Drill one ¾-inch hole in the drawer or door front to accommodate the trailer hitch.

Insert the trailer hitch through the hole.

Twist on the nut and tighten it until the hitch is held evenly in place (see Photo D).

A.

B.

C.

D.

the decorating pantry ▼

papers

Tour the scrapbook aisle of a crafts store or the art paper area of an art supply store, and you'll be amazed by how many decorative papers are available. Sometimes printed on one side, colorful papers are adorned with everything from basketballs to dahlias. **Natural fiber** and **handmade art papers** are the most expensive (some costing a few dollars or more per sheet); you may want to purchase a few of them to mix and match with more affordable papers. Use your favorites to decoupage a lamp base, an occasional table, a roller shade, or a picture frame. (Before you begin your decoupage project, rub decoupage glue on a small scrap of the decorative paper to make sure the paper won't bleed and that it will dry without wrinkling or bubbling.) You can also mat and frame the decorative paper itself to create instant art for a hallway, rec room, or guest bath.

You'll want to keep plenty of **tissue paper** on hand too. The newest versions are shimmering and colorful, and many are printed in attractive patterns. Use several layers of the translucent variety to make a quick cover for a less-than-stellar flowerpot or to add a decorative flourish around a clear-glass vase.

Of course, you'll never want to be without a package of **construction paper.** In addition to school projects, you can use this tried-and-true paper to frame your kid's best artwork or to create some colorful place mats for a backyard birthday party.

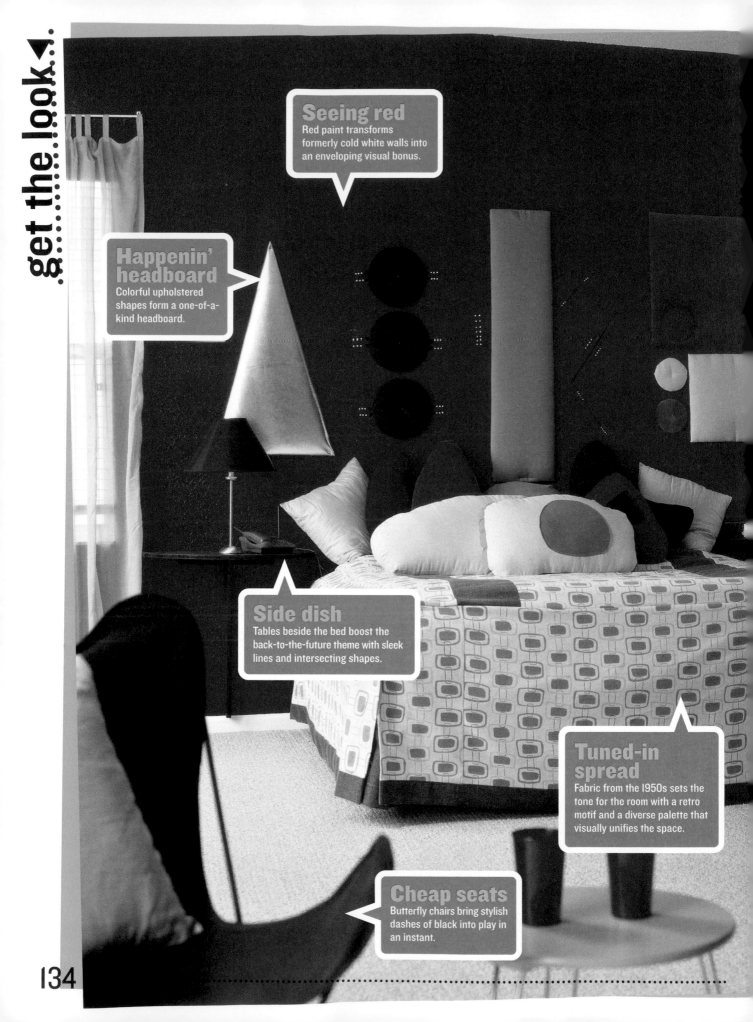

get the look ◀.

Seeing red
Red paint transforms formerly cold white walls into an enveloping visual bonus.

Happenin' headboard
Colorful upholstered shapes form a one-of-a-kind headboard.

Side dish
Tables beside the bed boost the back-to-the-future theme with sleek lines and intersecting shapes.

Tuned-in spread
Fabric from the 1950s sets the tone for the room with a retro motif and a diverse palette that visually unifies the space.

Cheap seats
Butterfly chairs bring stylish dashes of black into play in an instant.

When Frank first encountered this big bedroom, he playfully threw down bread crumbs to keep from getting lost. Style doesn't come up missing here, however, as bold red paint on the walls makes the cavernous space more intimate, and futuristic shapes spark a fun, retro atmosphere.

DESIGNED BY FRANK

shaping up

▶ Miramar: Avenue 164

This shot shows only a small portion of the featured king-size master bedroom. The homeowners feel the furniture and overall look of the space are out-of-date, and they ask Frank to modernize both but not to use pastels. They also point out that an alcove in the room is spacious enough to serve as a sitting area, where they could play video games and watch television.

T his episode could have been entitled "Rolling, Rolling, Rolling" because that's how Frank and the neighbors spend the bulk of their time: rolling coats of bright red paint onto the walls of an enormous master bedroom.

While the neighbors use rollers with extensions to apply two coats of red paint, Frank meticulously edge the tops of the walls with an artist's brush. "It's like painting the Sistine Chapel," he says.

The red makes the room cozy and inviting, but wall space as vast as this requires more interest than paint can provide. To stay on budget and on time, Frank fabricates a headboard out of various plywood shapes, wrapping them in batting and different solid fabrics to make them three-dimensional and colorful. Hook-and-loop tape makes hanging shapes like these a no-fuss job.

▲ Two simple shapes—a half-circle tabletop and a triangular base—form the modern bedside tables, which are screwed directly to the wall.

◀◀This dresser and mirror look stylish in fresh coats of black paint, set off against rich red walls. When painting white surfaces red, you will almost always need at least two coats to cover. Speed the process of painting an extra large space by inviting friends and family over for a paint party. Equip everyone with paint pans and hand out rollers with extension poles. Ask people with the steadiest hands to do the edging along the ceiling. If your walls and ceiling are smooth, you can make the edging process go faster by using a paint pad for this phase.

time crunch

▶ fast nightstands

The shapely nightstands used in this bedroom are fairly easy to make; you'll find even faster options on pages 36 and 37. Consider these other speedy night table solutions too:

▶ **PURCHASE STORAGE BOXES** from an office supply store or storage center. Paint the boxes or cover them with decorative paper. Stack them up beside the bed for storage and a place to stash a lamp and alarm clock.

▶ **SHOP FLEA MARKETS,** garage sales, and antiques malls to find vintage suitcases. Stack them beside the bed from largest to smallest. They're ideal for storing blankets and linens too.

▶ **TWO MATCHING** wicker wastebaskets can become a fast nightstand. Place one wastebasket normally on the floor. Flip the other wastebasket upside down and set its rim on top of the rim of the other wastebasket. Glue or wire the rims together. The bottom of the flipped basket becomes the tabletop. For a larger tabletop, glue on a wood table round (available at home centers). Finish the round as desired.

florist's wire

Why would you want this stuff cluttering up your pantry, you ask? Available in a range of widths and colors, the flexible wire provides all sorts of quick fixes, from holding up a drooping flower to wiring unsightly extension cords to the underside of a desk. It's perfect for attaching autumn flowers to a twig wreath or for wiring paper lanterns to porch columns. You can also use it to attach decorative baubles and ornaments to chandeliers, candelabra, and bedposts.

The paper-covered version of this handy wire is designed to protect against surface scratches, so it's perfect for creating temporary attachments such as wiring a holiday wreath to a door knocker. Because the paper-wrapped wire wraps and unwraps easily, you can also use it to organize pencils, cooking utensils, and plastic cutlery by wiring them into neat little bundles.

▼ Rather than invest a bundle in canvases, Frank found a pair of wood bifold doors for $27. He separated the sets, painted them black, added freehand designs, and hung the doors on the wall as art. Behind the bed, the colorful headboard shapes were a snap to install with hook-and-loop tape.

▶ The bedroom seems even more spacious now that this alcove sitting area is defined with a painted bifold door. Custom-built shelves, a pair of affordable butterfly chairs, and a small table make this an inviting spot to watch television and play video games.

◀ These shelves were custom-built. To save time purchase ready-made shelves and paint them. For a more contemporary look, consider using wire or wood closet components to shape a shelving unit for audiovisual equipment.

Complementing the funky style of the headboard is a bedspread fashioned from vintage fabric with a multicolor motif reminiscent of little televisions. Two stripes of solid-gray fabric—stitched into the topside of the bedspread—stretch the limited amount of fabric so it fits the bed beautifully. Whimsically shaped pillows in various colors pair up with bright yellow draperies to make the room lively and fun.

Butterfly chairs offer a comfortable place for enjoying the television and stereo now housed on custom-built, black-painted shelves that Frank designed with sexy, curving supports. The chairs require only minutes to unfold and set up on each side of a small occasional table.

For artwork, narrow wood panels (separated bifold doors) are painted black and decorated with small painted shapes and lines to suit the futuristic theme. An existing dresser and mirror are updated with a coat of black paint.

In the end, all the hours of painting pay off—the room is loaded with warmth and personality. Frank admits that all that rolling, rolling, rolling took its toll on everyone: "We were all going to go burn our paintbrushes when we were done," he says.

From the Designers

▶ **FRANK BIELEC**

Q What are the most common decorating problems you encounter in homes today?

A There are two problems I see:

ONE The objects in the room are out of scale. Decorative accessories and furniture are running too small, and I'm seeing a lot of the same-size stuff. I tell people to buy different sizes of decorative accessories to make the room more visually interesting. Also don't put a very small picture on a very large wall. Instead, do a grouping of pictures.

TWO The furniture goes right against the wall. People aren't utilizing the middle of the room. Push the pieces to the middle of the room—have fun and cut a sofa across a corner.

Q In addition to the home furnishings and accessories areas at discount stores, what other departments do you visit for decorating materials?

A The hardware and kitchen departments. You can find all kinds of neat art-oriented accessories in the kitchen department. For example, instead of hanging pictures, hang a grouping of great-looking plates. Put shelving up and do a display of dishes from the kitchen department. I like the hardware department to find new faucets and all sorts of stuff, such as plumbing supplies.

Q What are some fast fixes for cluttered, disorganized bookcases and shelves?

A Get rid of the stuff. Just box it up. You don't have to have everything you own on display. Take some things out that are sorted by a theme. Then box up the rest of the stuff as another theme. Take a Polaroid picture of the stuff in the box and slap the picture on the side of the box and store it. A picture is worth a thousand words. When you need a nice fresh room, you have your whole fresh bookshelf in a box just waiting for you.

home office
in a hurry

Computers and fax machines make it possible for many people to work from home. Children have more homework these days too. So it's no wonder many homeowners look for ways to squeeze a work desk project into the hours they have available. This desk project, which uses closet components readily available at home improvement stores, lets you create a desk that features the number of drawers and cubbies that you need and the correct amount of desktop space—all in a single weekend.

A.

Start with manufactured oak-slat shelving designed for creating closet storage.

1. **Surface solutions** Finish the sections as desired, using stain and clear polyurethane for a natural finish or primer and paint to suit your color palette (see Photo A).

2. **Work on wheels** Vertical shelving components are typically predrilled and can be assembled with pegs or screws in only a few minutes. To make a filing cabinet that will slip under a desk top, remove one tier from a 16-inch-wide three-tier storage unit. Screw casters to the bottom of the unit to make maneuvering the piece easy. Organize supplies and papers on the shelves with inexpensive file boxes (see Photo B).

3. **Find your niche** Lay one 12-inch-wide three-tier storage unit on its side on another same-size shelf to form this cubby wall storage. Use a pair of galvanized CD-drawers to elevate the cubbies above the desk top (see Photo C).

4. **All together now** Fashion the legs and top of the desk from 16-inch-wide shelves by cutting the shelves to the desired size and joining them with screws. Provide additional strength for the desk by adding L-brackets where each leg meets the desk top. Have a piece of glass cut to fit the top of the desk to serve as a solid writing surface. Wheel the filing cabinet underneath the desk to one side and top the desk with the CD drawers and the cubby wall storage.

B.

In a day

what you need

Materials
Manufactured oak-slat
  shelving designed for
  closet storage
Paint and primer or stain
  and polyurethane
Caster wheels
Decorative file boxes
Galvanized CD drawers
Metal L-brackets
Wood screws
Glass sized to fit desktop

Tools
Cordless drill

C.

▶ room
arrangin

You lug, push, and shove a heavy sofa to a spot in the room. Whew! Then you tug, nudge, and pull that big chair and ottoman into place. But, uh-oh, they don't fit there. Have you ever experienced this scenario? Save time and preserve energy for other projects by using this room arranging kit instead of muscle. Turn the page to learn how to arrange furniture templates on grid paper. You'll avoid having the it-doesn't-fit blues, and you'll pick up helpful tips and tricks to make all your arrangements more efficient and stylish.

g kit

Room arranging kits have been around for years because they save time and headaches. (They can also save your back. You're much less likely to try wedging a mammoth sectional sofa into a 3×4-foot window niche after seeing on paper that your brilliant furniture arrangement plan will never work.)

Using the *Trading Spaces* Room Arranging Kit is totally painless—and may even be a bit fun. Follow these steps to begin planning a new look for your spaces:

MEASURE YOUR SPACE Plot out the room or rooms you want to redo on a graph-paper grid. Use the grid on pages 152–153 or purchase grid paper from an office supply store. The recommended scale for grid paper is 1 square = 1 square foot.

▸ On a scrap piece of paper, draw a rough outline of your space; you'll soon add exact measurements. Indicate all windows, doors, and jogs in the walls.

▸ Pick one corner of the space to begin measuring.

▸ Measure from your starting corner to the first opening or window. Note this measurement on your sketch.

▸ As you encounter openings or windows, measure each one, including its surrounding woodwork. Note these measurements on your sketch.

▸ Measure the entire length of each wall and note the measurement in inches on the sketch. The measurements of wall segments and openings should add up to the length of the entire wall.

▸ Continue working your way around the room, noting all measurements on your sketch.

▸ Note the swing of any doors, casement windows, and cabinetry on your sketch.

▸ To ensure accuracy, remeasure your entire space. Better yet, have someone else measure the area. Double-check any discrepancies.

▸ Few rooms are perfectly square, so the lengths of opposite walls in a rectangular space may not match. However, if your numbers are off by more than an inch or two, you may have to do some creative carpentry if you plan to install flooring or baseboards, for example.

ADD ARCHITECTURAL DETAILS TO YOUR PLAN
Accurate placement of doors, windows, and other architectural features is one of the keys to making a redecorating project both functional and beautiful. Use the architectural symbols *below* to mark the position of such features on your plan so you can take the features into account when planning the design and placement of furniture .

▸ Use a different color to indicate architectural features.

▸ Use dotted lines to mark obstructions such as protruding ductwork, prominent light fixtures (such as chandeliers and ceiling fans), and angled ceilings.

▸ Using different colors, indicate outlets, light switches, cable connections, telephone jacks, and other important features.

USE THE FURNITURE TEMPLATES Trace or photocopy the appropriate pieces from the furniture templates on the following pages; then cut them out with a crafts knife or scissors. If you have furniture or special items that don't appear in the templates, measure them and then draw them to the same scale on grid paper—1 square = 1 square foot.

PLACE YOUR TEMPLATES ON THE GRID Now the fun begins! Move the templates around and mix up the look of your space. Does that armoire have to stand in the place it has stood for the last five years? Probably not. Refer to "Furniture Placement Tips and Tricks" on page 149 for great ideas.

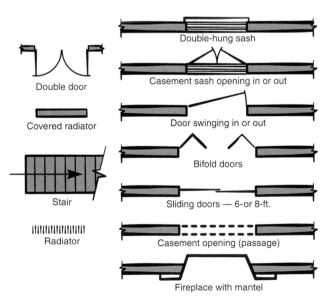

Double door

Covered radiator

Stair

Radiator

Double-hung sash

Casement sash opening in or out

Door swinging in or out

Bifold doors

Sliding doors — 6-or 8-ft.

Casement opening (passage)

Fireplace with mantel

Reclining chair
30×29 (opens to 66)

Headrest

Footrest

Sofa bed
35×75-92

Opens to
this size

Sofa bed
35×70-82

Opens to
this size

Sofa
32×72-78-84-90-96-102

Overstuffed sofa
36×72-78-84-90-96-102

Love seat
32×50-55-60

Overstuffed
love seat
36×50-55-60

Daybed
96×45

Barrel
chair
30×30

Lounge
chair
30×30

Lounge
chair
32×32

Wing
chair
33×34

Ottoman
32×32

Right-arm
module
32×32

Armless
module
32×32

Left-arm
module
32×32

Ottoman
22×22

Ottoman
20×27

Ottoman
16×30

Occasional chair
24×20

Occasional chair
25×20

Occasional chair
26×22

Armchair
27×27

Armchair
29×27

Rocking chair
22×24

Round
ottoman
32"

Chaise
lounge
24×60

King-size
with headboard
80×83

Mattress
80×78

Queen-size
with headboard
80×64

Mattress
80×60

Double bed
with headboard
75×59

Mattress
75×54

Twin bed
with headboard
75×44

Mattress
75×39

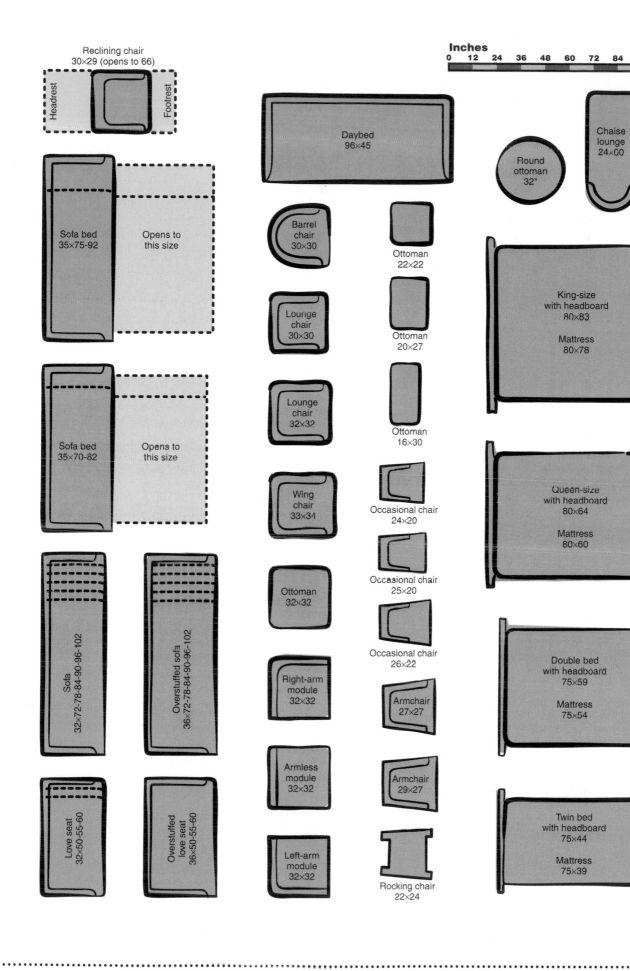

In Scott Air Force Base: Ash Creek Road, Kia strategically arranged the furniture in a narrow living/dining room to create two separate areas. The red slipcovered sofa divides the room like an upholstered half-wall, offering a clean visual break between the dining area (visible behind the sofa, *above left*) and the cozy conversation cluster in the living area.

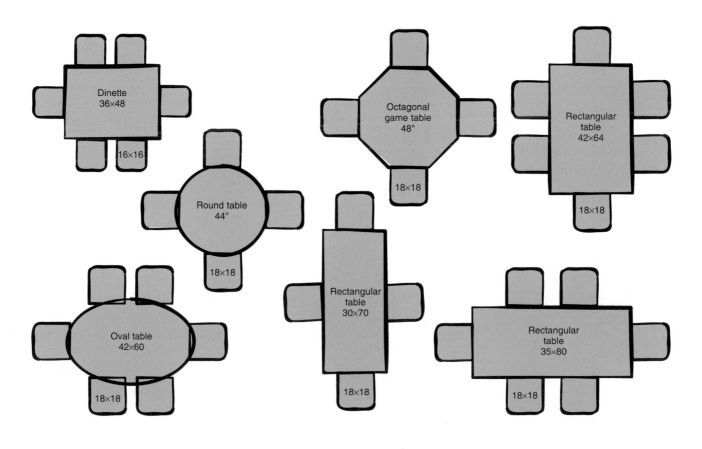

Dinette
36×48

16×16

Round table
44"

18×18

Oval table
42×60

18×18

Octagonal
game table
48"

18×18

Rectangular
table
30×70

18×18

Rectangular
table
42×64

18×18

Rectangular
table
35×80

18×18

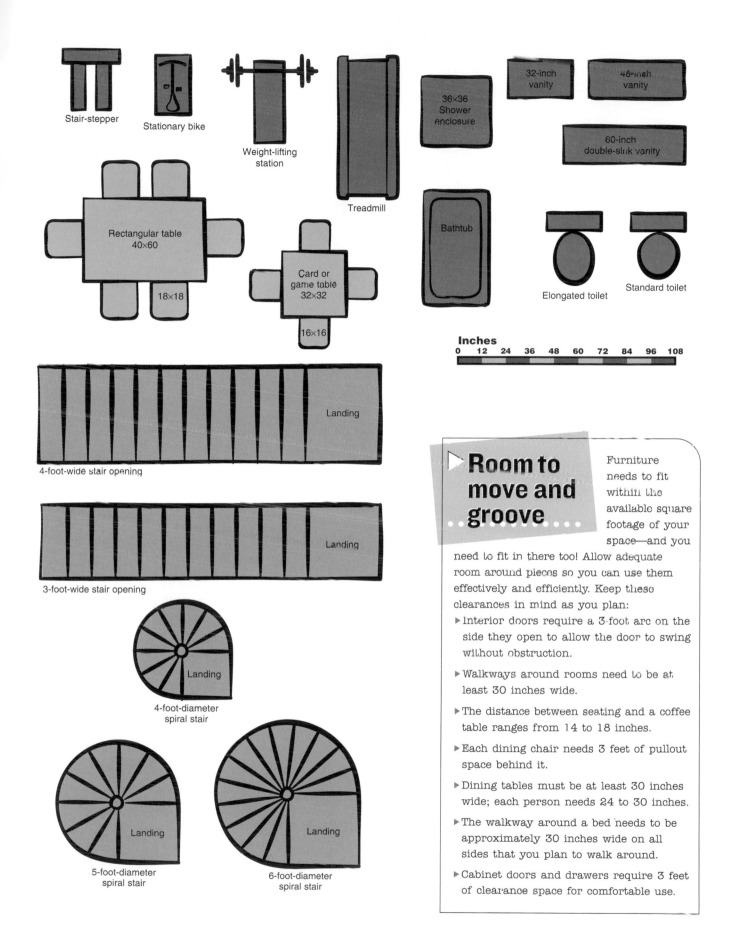

Stair-stepper

Stationary bike

Weight-lifting station

Treadmill

Rectangular table 40×60

18×18

Card or game table 32×32

16×16

36×36 Shower enclosure

Bathtub

32-inch vanity

48-inch vanity

60-inch double-sink vanity

Elongated toilet

Standard toilet

Inches

0   12   24   36   48   60   72   84   96   108

Landing

4-foot-wide stair opening

Landing

3-foot-wide stair opening

Landing

4-foot-diameter spiral stair

Landing

5-foot-diameter spiral stair

Landing

6-foot-diameter spiral stair

▶ Room to move and groove

Furniture needs to fit within the available square footage of your space—and you need to fit in there too! Allow adequate room around pieces so you can use them effectively and efficiently. Keep these clearances in mind as you plan:

▶ Interior doors require a 3-foot arc on the side they open to allow the door to swing without obstruction.

▶ Walkways around rooms need to be at least 30 inches wide.

▶ The distance between seating and a coffee table ranges from 14 to 18 inches.

▶ Each dining chair needs 3 feet of pullout space behind it.

▶ Dining tables must be at least 30 inches wide; each person needs 24 to 30 inches.

▶ The walkway around a bed needs to be approximately 30 inches wide on all sides that you plan to walk around.

▶ Cabinet doors and drawers require 3 feet of clearance space for comfortable use.

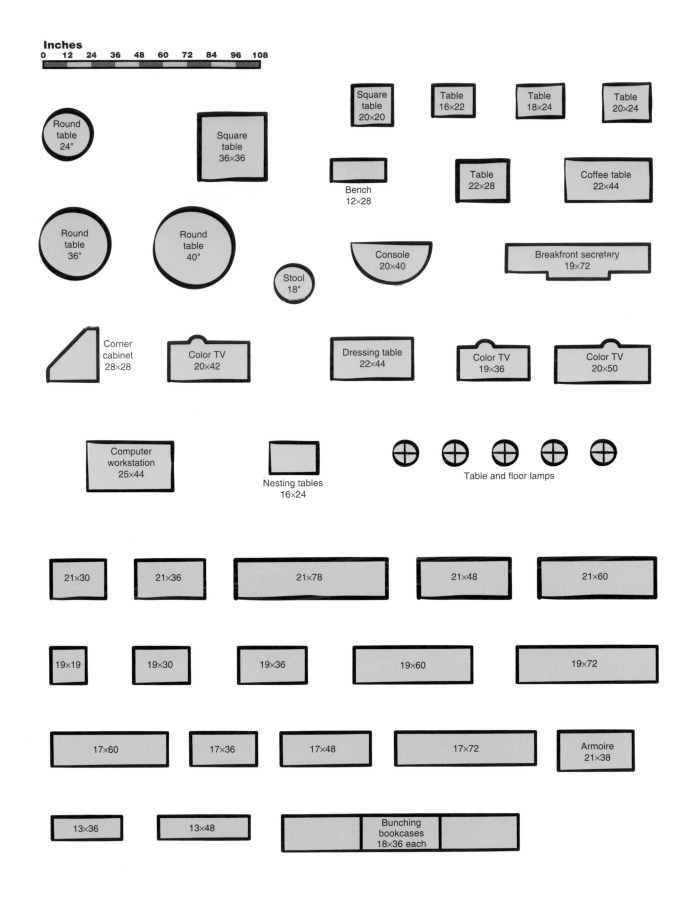

Inches

0 12 24 36 48 60 72 84 96 108

Round table 24"

Square table 36×36

Square table 20×20

Table 16×22

Table 18×24

Table 20×24

Bench 12×28

Table 22×28

Coffee table 22×44

Round table 36"

Round table 40"

Stool 18"

Console 20×40

Breakfront secretary 19×72

Corner cabinet 28×28

Color TV 20×42

Dressing table 22×44

Color TV 19×36

Color TV 20×50

Computer workstation 25×44

Nesting tables 16×24

Table and floor lamps

21×30

21×36

21×78

21×48

21×60

19×19

19×30

19×36

19×60

19×72

17×60

17×36

17×48

17×72

Armoire 21×38

13×36

13×48

Bunching bookcases 18×36 each

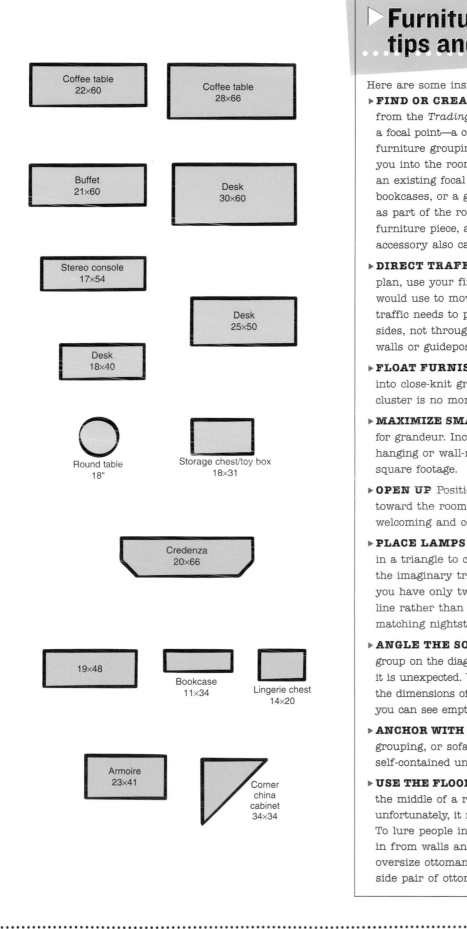

Coffee table
22×60

Coffee table
28×66

Buffet
21×60

Desk
30×60

Stereo console
17×54

Desk
25×50

Desk
18×40

Round table
18"

Storage chest/toy box
18×31

Credenza
20×66

19×48

Bookcase
11×34

Lingerie chest
14×20

Armoire
23×41

Corner
china
cabinet
34×34

Here are some insider tips for planning stylish spaces:

▶ **FIND OR CREATE A FOCAL POINT** Take a cue from the *Trading Spaces* crew: Each space needs a focal point—a cornerstone on which to build a furniture grouping, a dramatic element that draws you into the room. If your space doesn't have an existing focal point, such as a fireplace, built-in bookcases, or a great window, consider adding one as part of the room makeover. A large-scale furniture piece, a bold piece of art, or a stunning accessory also can serve as a focal point.

▶ **DIRECT TRAFFIC** After you place furniture on your plan, use your finger to trace the paths that people would use to move within and through the space. If traffic needs to pass through a space, direct it to the sides, not through the center. Think of furnishings as walls or guideposts that funnel traffic.

▶ **FLOAT FURNISHINGS** Pull pieces away from walls into close-knit groups. Make sure any seat within a cluster is no more than 8 feet apart from the others.

▶ **MAXIMIZE SMALL SPACES** Include a large piece for grandeur. Incorporate vertical storage and hanging or wall-mounted light fixtures to maximize square footage.

▶ **OPEN UP** Position seating groups so they open up toward the room entrance. The space will feel more welcoming and cozy.

▶ **PLACE LAMPS STRATEGICALLY** Position lamps in a triangle to create a balanced look (the sides of the imaginary triangle can be different lengths). If you have only two lamps, place them on a diagonal line rather than on each end of a sofa or on matching nightstands.

▶ **ANGLE THE SOFA** Placing the sofa and the seating group on the diagonal instantly adds interest because it is unexpected. Your eye is tricked into believing that the dimensions of the room are more generous because you can see empty space beyond the furniture.

▶ **ANCHOR WITH RUGS** Make a dining set, conversation grouping, or sofa and coffee table combo feel like a self-contained unit by grounding the pieces on a rug.

▶ **USE THE FLOOR SPACE** You might think that leaving the middle of a room empty would create openness; unfortunately, it merely promotes a cavernous feeling. To lure people in and create interest, pull furniture in from walls and create a hub at the center with an oversize ottoman, a large coffee table, or a side-by-side pair of ottomans or coffee tables.

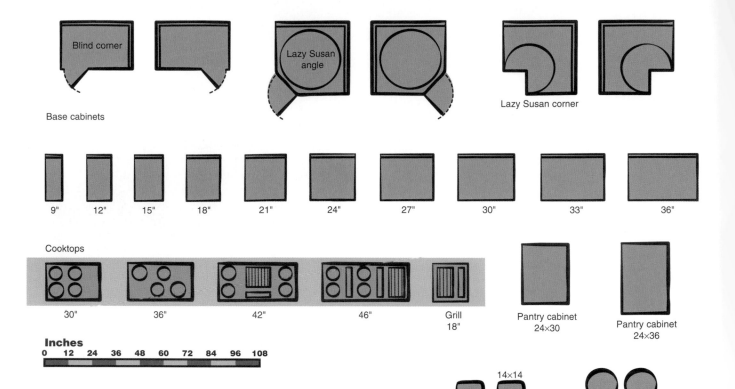

Base cabinets

Blind corner

Lazy Susan angle

Lazy Susan corner

9" 12" 15" 18" 21" 24" 27" 30" 33" 36"

Cooktops

30" 36" 42" 46" Grill 18"

Pantry cabinet 24×30

Pantry cabinet 24×36

Inches

0 12 24 36 48 60 72 84 96 108

14×14

Work island 24×43

Stool 15"

▶ Some other common furniture measurements

▶ Most new upholstered furniture is more generously sized than earlier styles. Sofas range in widths of approximately 70 to 102 inches. Common depths for upholstered furniture range from 35 to 40 inches. If square footage is at a premium, look for smaller-scale upholstered pieces from the 1940s through 1970s at flea markets, garage sales, and vintage stores.

▶ Bookcases are typically 9 to 12 inches deep. Bookcases with measurements above or below this range are rare and often require custom building.

▶ Two-drawer filing cabinets run approximately 29"H×15"W×28½"D for letter-size drawers; 29"H×18¼"W×28½"D for legal-size drawers.

▶ Windowsills are typically 18 to 36 inches from the floor. Ottomans, benches, and cube storage are best options for furniture in front of windows; low-back upholstered pieces are also a good choice.

▶ Standard kitchen cabinets typically measure 24 inches deep and come in widths of 9, 12, 15, 18, 21, 24, 27, 30, 33, and 36 inches.

Sinks

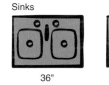

36" 48" 30"

Drop-in range 27" Drop-in range 30" Freestanding range 30" Freestanding range 36"

Microwave ovens

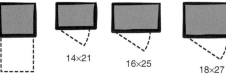

14×21 16×25 18×27

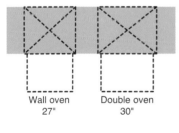

Wall oven
27"

Double oven
30"

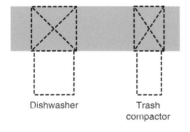

Dishwasher

Trash
compactor

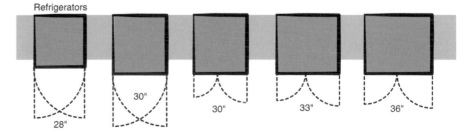

Refrigerators

28"

30"

30"

33"

36"

To boost the intimacy of a giant master bedroom, Frank pulled the furniture into the center of the room, filling the cathedral-ceilinged space with weighty pieces and gauzy drapery. The rustic four-poster bed, *above*, is positioned near the center of the room, a restful island oasis for the homeowners. By including a coffee bar in the room, *left*, Frank indulges one of the homeowner's interests. The bar, positioned at a diagonal, fills an empty space in the corner and offers easy access to the java-making supplies stored beneath the countertop.

▶ Photocopy this grid at its original size or purchase
¼-inch grid paper from an office supply store. Then
photocopy and cut out the templates on pages
145–151 to begin laying out your new space. The
grid scale is 1 square = 1 square foot.

Inches

0   12   24   36   48   60   72   84   96   108

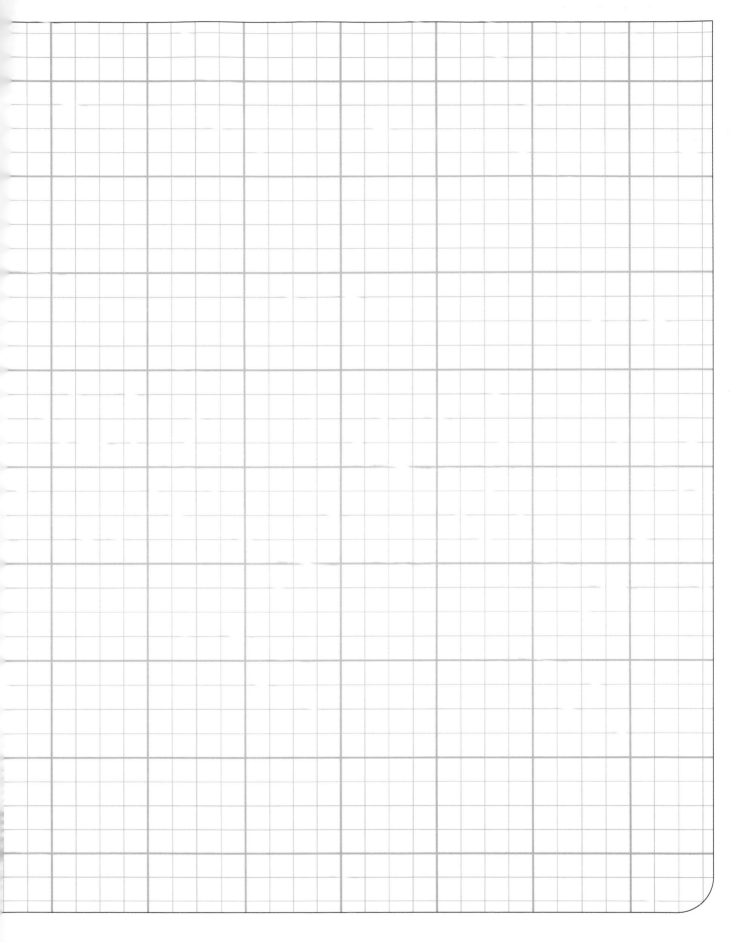

episode guide

You already know that each episode of *Trading Spaces* is absolutely bursting with fantastic decorating inspiration for every budget and style. But how can you possibly keep track of all those hundreds of rooms and projects?

Fret no more, fans! Consider the following sections your personal *Trading Spaces* programming guide.

▶ **THE EPISODE GUIDE** that begins below chronologically lists and describes every *Trading Spaces* episode, Seasons I through 3.

▶ **THE DECORATING IDEA INDEX** that begins on page 168 helps you identify episodes in the list that match your specific decorating needs in terms of room type, colors used, major projects, themes, and more.

For more information and helpful before and after photos from each episode, check out *Trading Spaces Ultimate Episode Guide* (©2003, Meredith Books) or visit http://tlc.discovery.com/fansites/tradingspaces/tradingspaces.html.

Who knew watching television could be so inspiring?

Season 1

E1: Knoxville, TN: Fourth & Gill
Cast: Alex, Frank, Laurie, Amy Wynn
In the premiere episode, Frank brightens a den by using a faux-suede finish in shades of gold on the walls, reupholstering the homeowners' Arts and Crafts furniture, and painting two armoires in shades of red, gold, and black. Laurie punches up a bland kitchen by painting the walls electric pear, retiling the floor in large black and white checks, and using chrome accents. She also creates an organized family message and filing center.

E2: Knoxville, TN: Forest Glen
Cast: Alex, Doug, Hildi, Amy Wynn
Doug creates a romantic bedroom, which he titles "Country Urbane," by painting the walls sage green, building an upholstered bed, pickling (whitewashing) an existing vanity, and making a privacy screen. Hildi designs a

sleek living room, painting the walls a dark putty color and a thin black stripe around the edge of the wood floor, sewing white slipcovers and curtains, hanging spotlights on the walls to showcase the homeowners' art, and building end tables that spin on lazy Susans.

E3: Athens, GA: County Road
Cast: Alex, Frank, Hildi, Amy Wynn
Frank brightens a child's room by painting the walls lavender, hanging a swing from the ceiling, making a wall-size art area with chalkboard spray paint, and spray-painting a mural of white trees. Hildi updates a kitchen/living room area by painting the dark wood paneling and ceiling ecru, hanging cream draperies, slipcovering chairs with monkey-print fabric, building shelves to showcase the homeowners' pewter collection, enlarging the dining area by ripping out a portion of the carpet and laying vinyl tiles, and painting several pieces of furniture black.

E4: Alpharetta, GA: Providence Oaks
Cast: Alex, Hildi, Roderick, Amy Wynn
Hildi re-creates a dining room using the existing dining table, aubergine paint, horizontal wall stripes of a high-gloss glaze, pistachio-color curtains, two-tone slipcovers, a striking star-shape light fixture, and a privacy screen. Roderick brightens a den/guest room by painting off-white stripes on the existing khaki walls, stenciling a sun motif in a deep rust-red, slipcovering the furniture with an off-white fabric, and installing a wall-length desk that can be hidden with curtains.

E5: Lawrenceville, GA: Pine Lane
Cast: Alex, Dez, Hildi, Amy Wynn
Dez adds a feminine touch to a dark wood-paneled living room by whitewashing the walls, painting the fireplace, and dismantling a banister. She finds new ways to display the husband's taxidermy and decoy duck

collection, which includes a custom duck lamp. Hildi brings the outdoors in, creating an organically hip living room with a tree limb valance, wicker furniture, minty-white walls, and an armoire covered with dried leaves.

E6: Buckhead, GA: Canter Road
Cast: Alex, Genevieve, Laurie, Amy Wynn
Gen gets wild in a kitchen by painting the walls electric pear, adding silver accents, using colanders as light covers, painting the existing formica counter top brown, and removing cabinet doors. Laurie creates a crisp living room by painting the walls chocolate brown, laying a sea-grass rug, hanging a white frame on a large mirror, and adding cream and white slipcovers and curtains.

E7: Washington, D.C.: Cleveland Park
Cast: Alex, Dez, Doug, Ty
Dez creates a funky-festive living room by combining electric pear, white, gray, black, and red paint in solids, stripes, polka dots, and textured faux finishes. She adds unusual lighting to the room by building a three-headed Medusa lamp complete with spiky lightbulbs and Christmas lights. Doug goes retro in a basement by making a beanbag sofa and a kidney-shape coffee table with legs made of plastic tumblers. He also paints the walls bright orange stenciled with white geometric shapes.

E8: Alexandria, VA: Riefton Court
Cast: Alex, Frank, Genevieve, Ty
Frank cozies a country kitchen by creating a picket-fence shelving unit and using seven pastel paint colors to create a hand-painted quilt on the walls. Gen goes graphic in a living room, enlarging and recropping family photos, turning an existing entertainment center on its side, and painting the walls bright red.

E9: Annapolis, MD: Fox Hollow
Cast: Alex, Genevieve, Laurie, Ty
Gen warms a living room with butterscotch paint, white curtains, framed family pictures, and a combination wood/carpet floor. Laurie enlivens a drab kitchen with muted pumpkin paint, new light fixtures, and a custom pot hanger.

E10: Philadelphia, PA: Strathmore Road
Cast: Alex, Dez, Frank, Amy Wynn
Frank goes earthy by painting a living room brown with a sueding technique. He also creates handmade accents, a child-size tepee, and a window seat with storage. Dez tries for "casual elegance" in a living room, using purple paint, a repeated gray harlequin diamond pattern on the walls, and an end table lamp made out of a trash can.

E11: Philadelphia, PA: Valley Road
Cast: Alex, Doug, Laurie, Amy Wynn
Doug softens a sunroom he names "Blue Lagoon" by painting the walls a deep robin's egg blue, painting blue and white diamonds on the hardwood floor, hanging

Doug's Room
Valley Road, Philadelphia, PA

whitewashed bamboo blinds, and adding pale yellow accents. He adds a *Rear Window* touch by placing a pair of binoculars (which he finds in the basement) in the sunroom so the homeowners can watch their children playing outside. Laurie goes Greek, painting a living room deep russet with black and white accents, adding white Grecian urns, and even creating a white bust using one of her homeowners as a model.

E12: Philadelphia, PA: Galahad Road
Cast: Alex, Genevieve, Hildi, Amy Wynn
Hildi warms a family-friendly living/dining room by introducing coffee-color walls, a midnight blue fireplace, a custom-built sectional couch, and zebra-stripe dining chair covers. Gen brightens a basement den by painting the walls lily pad green, adding orange accents, installing a white modern couch, and weaving white fabric on the ceiling to cover the drop-ceiling tiles.

E13: Knoxville, TN: Courtney Oak
Cast: Alex, Frank, Laurie, Amy Wynn
Frank gets in touch with his "inner child" by painting the walls of a basement light denim blue, freehanding murals of trees and flowers, and spray-painting fluffy white clouds. Laurie goes organic by painting a bedroom a deep pistachio green, adding soft draperies, painting a vine around the vanity mirror, and using a cornice board to drape fabric on either side of the headboard.

E14: Cincinnati, OH: Melrose Avenue
Cast: Alex, Frank, Hildi, Ty
Frank adds soft Victorian touches to a living room by exposing the existing wood floor, creating a faux-tin fireplace surround, painting a navy wall border with a rose motif, creating a fireplace screen that matches the border, and building a bench-style coffee table. Hildi gets crafty in a kitchen, creating her own wallpaper with tissue paper and flower stencils based on a fabric pattern. She installs a found dishwasher, extends the countertop, builds an island out of the kitchen table, paints the ceiling and the furniture yellow, and lays vinyl tile flooring.

E15: Cincinnati, OH: Sturbridge Road
Cast: Alex, Doug, Genevieve, Ty
Gen creates an Indian bedroom for a teenage girl by painting the walls with warm golden and red tones,

hanging a beaded curtain, and creating a draped canopy. Doug turns a dining room into a "Zen-Buddhist-Asian room" with a chocolate brown ceiling, warm honey-copper walls, Venetian plaster squares, a distressed wooden dining table, and folded-metal-screen window treatments.

E16: Cincinnati, OH: Madison & Forest
Cast: Alex, Doug, Laurie, Ty
Doug transforms a Victorian living room into an industrial loft with multiple shades of purple paint, a yellow ceiling, custom art made from coordinating paint chips, wall sconces made of candy dishes, and a chair reupholstered in Holstein-print fabric. Laurie warms a tiny bedroom with mustard yellow paint, a custom-built entertainment center, and a short suspended bed canopy.

E17: San Diego, CA: Elm Ridge
Cast: Alex, Genevieve, Hildi, Amy Wynn
In this infamous episode, Gen truly brings the outdoors in: She covers a bedroom wall with Oregon moss, lays a natural-tone tile floor, and adds a canopy that is lit from above with twinkling lights. Hildi works to convince her homeowners that they can brighten a bedroom by painting the walls and furniture black, adding zebra-stripe floor cubes, creating a copper-mesh bust to display in the room, and using exposed subflooring in place of carpet.

E18: San Diego, CA: Hermes Avenue
Cast: Alex, Genevieve, Laurie, Amy Wynn
Laurie brightens a kitchen by painting the walls Tiffany-box blue, installing a wooden slat grid system on one wall, hanging butter yellow draperies, building a banquette seating area, coating the stove in chrome-color paint, and painting the cabinets butter yellow. Gen uses Georgia O'Keeffe's Southwestern paintings as inspiration for transforming a living room. She paints the walls clay red, hangs a cow skull above the fireplace, adds a woven rug, hangs new light fixtures, frames large black and white cropped photos of the homeowners' children, builds a distressed coffee table with firewood legs, and covers the existing baby bumpers with crafts fur.

E19: San Diego, CA: Wilbur Street
Cast: Alex, Doug, Frank, Amy Wynn
Frank mixes British Colonial and tropical looks in a living room with soft mauve paint, exposed wood flooring, several flowerpots and vases, and a custom architectural piece. Doug updates a dark kitchen with a "Tuscan Today" theme, using Venetian plaster tinted "Tuscan Mango" (OK, it's orange), painting the cabinets white and orange, and installing wood flooring.

E20: Knoxville, TN: Stubbs Bluff
Cast: Alex, Doug, Frank, Ty
Doug brings a farmhouse kitchen up-to-date by painting the walls a muted coffee color, adding sage and lilac accents, building benches in the dining area, hanging

silver cooking utensils on the painted cabinet fronts and a shovel and pitchfork painted white on the wall, and laying vinyl tile. He titles his room "Cocteau Country." Frank lets the ideas flow while punching up a basement with a karaoke stage, a tiki hut bar, and several other tropical accents—including a canoe for seating.

E21: Miami, FL: 168th/83rd Streets
Cast: Alex, Dez, Laurie, Ty
Laurie warms up a living room by painting the walls brick red with black and cream accents, building two large bookcases, hanging botanical prints, slipcovering the existing furniture, and using a faux-tortoiseshell finish on a coffee table. Dez adds drama to a bedroom by applying a "pan-Asian ethnic theme" featuring upholstered cornice boards, mosquito netting, and stenciled dragon lampshades.

E22: Fort Lauderdale, FL: 59th Street
Cast: Alex, Frank, Hildi, Ty
Frank adds "comfortable drama" to a living room with bright orange textured walls, a mosaic-top coffee table, slipcovered furniture, and a large custom art project made from three wooden doors. Hildi goes retro in a Fiestaware collector's kitchen by building an acrylic table, adding period chairs, and hanging large globe light fixtures. She also installs a shelving unit to display the homeowner's collection.

E23: Key West, FL: Elizabeth Street
Cast: Alex, Frank, Genevieve, Ty
Frank adds a Caribbean touch to a living room by painting the walls light blue, adding a hand-painted mermaid, building a telephone table, and laying vinyl tiles. Gen makes a tiny living room appear larger with her "Caribbean Chill" design, which includes magenta walls with lime green accents, a large custom-built sectional sofa, and a wall decoupaged with pages torn from a 100-year-old book.

E24: Austin, TX: Wycliff
Cast: Alex, Doug, Hildi, Amy Wynn
Doug creates a funky kitchen by painting the cabinets with blue and purple swirls, extending the existing countertop, applying blue and purple vinyl squares on the wall, and hanging numerous clocks (he titles the room "Time Flies"). Hildi adds drama to a dining room by covering the walls with brown felt, papering the ceiling with small, individual red and gold squares, covering the back of an armoire with dried bamboo leaves, and making custom light fixtures.

E25: Austin, TX: Wing Road
Cast: Alex, Genevieve, Hildi, Amy Wynn
Gen goes south of the border in a kitchen by adding a mosaic tile backsplash, covering the cabinet door insets with textured tin, painting the floors a terra-cotta color, and painting the walls yellow. She also uses colanders as light fixtures and covers a barstool with a tall pasta pot. Hildi brightens a living room by applying a textured glaze over the existing gold paint, covering a wall in wooden squares, sewing silver slipcovers, and adding a cowhide rug.

E26: Austin, TX: Birdhouse Drive
Cast: Alex, Frank, Laurie, Amy Wynn
Frank enlivens a living room by painting three walls sage green, painting the fireplace wall shocking pink, installing floor-to-ceiling shelving on either side of the fireplace, adding a hand-painted checkerboard table, and making unique art pieces. Laurie divides a living/dining room with a suspended piece of fabric, paints the rooms with warm oranges and yellows, adds olive green accents, builds a bench seat, and creates a custom coffee table.

E27: Orlando, FL: Lake Catherine
Cast: Alex, Hildi, Vern, Ty
Vern brings warmth and depth into a wine importer's kitchen by painting the walls with two shades of red, installing a custom-built wine rack, building a new chandelier using 36 wineglasses, and creating a new tabletop. Hildi creates a sleek bedroom with gray walls, an aluminum foil ceiling, gray flannel curtains, bamboo curtain rods, and a black armoire covered in bamboo. She also includes a live canary in her design and names the bird "Hildi."

E28: Orlando, FL: Gotha Furlong
Cast: Alex, Frank, Genevieve, Ty
Gen creates romance in a bedroom by adding a ceiling-height cedar plank headboard, butter yellow paint, throw pillows made from a 1970s tablecloth, and cedar bookshelves. Frank makes a bedroom feel "earthy, arty, and wonderful" by painting the walls tan, adding gauzy white fabric to the four-poster bed, building a cedar window seat with storage drawers, painting a floorcloth, and hand painting batik-print pillows.

E29: Orlando, FL: Winterhaven
Cast: Alex, Doug, Laurie, Ty
Laurie perks up a seldom used living room with yellow paint, sheer window treatments, a geometric wall design, and a large ottoman. Doug regresses to his childhood while decorating a boy's bedroom. Doug's design, "Americana Medley," includes red walls, a blue ceiling, stenciled stars and cow prints, a tree limb headboard, and a barn door window treatment.

E30: Albuquerque, NM: Gloria
Cast: Alex, Doug, Hildi, Ty
Hildi warms up a living room by painting the walls brown and copper, applying yellow fabric paint to the existing furniture, making a curtain rod from copper pipe, and installing an entertainment center. Doug sets sail in a

Laurie's Room
Winterhaven, Orlando, FL

living room ("Wind in Our Sails") by painting the walls slate gray, hanging white curtains, installing a banquette, and suspending a large white canvas from the ceiling.

E31: Santa Fe, NM: Felize
Cast: Alex, Genevieve, Vern, Ty
Gen designs a modern Southwestern living room ("Adobe Mod") by adding white paint, a custom-built sofa, woven-rope end tables, and clay jars. Vern creates a calming oasis in a kitchen by painting the walls pale blue, installing a planter of wheat grass, laying parquet flooring, hanging mirrors, and applying a stained-glass-looking treatment to the cabinet doors.

E32: New Orleans, LA: Jacob Street
Cast: Alex, Hildi, Laurie, Amy Wynn
Laurie creates continuity and flow in a kitchen/office/dining/living room, using pale yellow paint on the walls, a 20-foot-long sisal rug, slipcovers, new kitchen storage, and a new furniture arrangement. Hildi modernizes a kitchen by painting the walls pistachio green, laying black vinyl tile, building a new island, and using plumbing conduit as shelving supports.

E33: New Orleans, LA: Walter Road
Cast: Alex, Frank, Genevieve, Amy Wynn
Gen creates an antique look in a bedroom she titles "Bombay Meets Étouffée." She paints the walls peach and pea green, installs a vintage beaded chandelier, and applies an antiqued gold finish to cornice boards and bookshelves. Frank updates a kitchen by removing garish wallpaper, coating the walls with textured tan paint, painting the cabinet drawers red and green, coiling copper wire around the existing drawer pulls, and installing a large bulletin board to help keep the family organized.

E34: New Orleans, LA: D'evereaux Street
Cast: Alex, Genevieve, Vern, Amy Wynn
Vern kicks up the style in a bedroom shared by two young brothers with a black and white soccer theme. He paints

after

Hildi's Room
Quakers Way, Quakertown, PA

the walls black and white, upholsters the headboards, creates two desk stations, suspends soccer balls from the ceiling, and lays a black and white vinyl floor complete with a custom soccer ball medallion. Gen heads back to the 1960s in her "Retro Fly" den/guest room by painting multicolor stripes on the walls, hanging retro light fixtures, slipcovering an existing futon, and separating the desk area from the seating area with a chain-link screen.

E35: New York: Shore Road
Cast: Alex, Dez, Genevieve, Amy Wynn
Gen looks to the East for inspiration on a sunporch and creates a tearoom atmosphere with a new sake bar, a seating area, and several organic accents. Dez gives a living room her version of "country with a French twist" by painting the walls yellow, stenciling fern leaves around the room, slipcovering the existing sofa, adding a planter of grass, and hanging geometric window treatments.

E36: New York: Sherwood Drive
Cast: Alex, Doug, Vern, Amy Wynn
Vern creates a serene bedroom by painting the walls lilac-blue, making a television cabinet out of picture frames, hanging yards of indigo-color velvet, installing sconces containing live Beta fish above the bed, and creating a 4-foot-diameter wall clock out of candle sconces and battery-operated clock hands. Doug designs a relaxing "Zen-sational" bedroom by hanging grass cloth on the walls, making light fixtures out of Malaysian baskets, hanging a full-length mirror on an angle, and building a 6-foot-tall fountain.

E37: New York: Linda Court
Cast: Alex, Doug, Frank, Amy Wynn
Doug creates a Mediterranean-flavor living room by covering the walls in yellow Venetian plaster, making custom lamps, building a large armoire to match an existing one, and weaving strips of wood through metal conduit for a woven-wall effect. Frank also heads to the Mediterranean in a living room, applying a faux finish with three shades of

yellow paint, then adding stenciled squares on the walls, a faux fresco created from drywall, and gondola-inspired lamps. He titles his room "Mediterranean Trust Me."

E38: New Jersey: Sam Street
Cast: Alex, Hildi, Laurie, Ty
Laurie warms up a dining room with yellow paint, shades of pink as accents, a custom-built cornice board, and cream paint on the existing furniture. Hildi adds drama and romance to a bedroom by painting the walls a yellowed sage green, bringing in several sage silk fabrics, adding a sofa upholstered in burgundy fabric, extending the existing headboard, and building "pillow pod" seating.

E39: New Jersey: Lincroft
Cast: Alex, Doug, Laurie, Ty
Laurie adds style and function to a small kitchen by laying parquet vinyl flooring, painting the walls an ocher yellow, wall-mounting the microwave oven, painting the cabinets white, and creating a home office/family message center. Doug softens a very red living room by painting the walls sandy taupe, adding wooden strips to accentuate the ceiling height, painting colorful checkerboard designs on coffee tables, sewing several brightly colored rag rugs together to create a large carpet, and designing a wooden candleholder using a rope-and pulley system. He titles the look "Country Kaleidoscope."

E40: New Jersey: Lafayette Street
Cast: Alex, Frank, Vern, Ty
Frank adds Victorian elements to a dining/living room by painting the walls pink with burgundy accents, showcasing the homeowners' collection of wooden houses, applying decorative molding to the existing entertainment center, and creating original wall art using basic wood-carving skills. Vern creates a baby-friendly living room. He paints the walls two shades of sage green, builds a large upholstered ottoman that doubles as a coffee table, builds a sofa out of a mattress, suspends a mantel for the fireplace, and adds bright blue accents. He also enlarges pictures of the homeowners' baby and uses them as lampshades on three wall lamps.

Season 2

E1: Quakertown, PA: Quakers Way
Cast: Paige, Doug, Hildi, Ty
Doug goes "ball-istic" in a living room, painting the walls lime green, building a custom sofa complete with bowling ball feet, hanging a wall of mirrors, making custom lamps out of gazing balls, and adding brown and blue accents. Hildi introduces viewers to the concept of orthogonal design by painting perpendicular lines on the walls and ceiling of a basement, creating a nine-piece sectional seating area,

hanging three acrylic box frames filled with different types of candy, and screening off a large storage area.

E2: New Jersey: Tall Pines Drive
Cast: Paige, Laurie, Vern, Amy Wynn
Laurie uses several paint colors in a basement to create a large Matisse-inspired mural. She also makes a chalkboard-top kids' table, installs an art station, creates curtains out of place mats, and hangs louvered panels as a room screen. Vern designs a love nest in a bedroom by hanging brown upholstered wall squares, sewing lush draperies using several yards of brown fabric, painting the existing furniture white, installing silver candle chandeliers, and adding new bedside tables.

E3: Maple Glen, PA: Fiedler Road
Cast: Paige, Genevieve, Laurie, Amy Wynn
Laurie paints the walls of a bedroom celadon green, creates a headboard from white and yellow silk squares, paints the existing furniture white, installs bamboo pieces as door hardware, and converts bamboo place mats into pillow shams. Using lillies as inspiration in a living room, Gen paints the walls a yellowed taupe, builds two new couches and a new coffee table, hangs large black and white family photos, and pins prints of vintage botanical postcards to the wall.

E4: Northampton, PA: James Avenue
Cast: Paige, Frank, Hildi, Ty
Hildi updates a living room with mustard-gold paint, aubergine curtains, yellow and red tufted pillows, a sisal rug, silk sunflowers, and a river rock mosaic fireplace. Frank creates a nautical Nantucket theme in a living room by painting the walls pale sage, adding yellow and seafoam green pillows, wrapping rope around the coffee table legs to make the table resemble a pier, and building a dinghy-inspired dog bed.

E5: Providence, RI: Phillips Street
Cast: Paige, Hildi, Vern, Amy Wynn
Hildi adds sophistication to a living room by painting the walls slate gray, making butter yellow slipcovers, adding a touch of charcoal wax to an existing coffee table and side tables, removing the existing ceiling fan, and replacing the drop-ceiling tiles with wood-tone panels. She also creates a child's table with decoupaged drawings of kids holding hands. Vern uses the principles of *feng shui* in a living room by painting the walls and ceiling yellow for wealth, designing a coffee table that holds bamboo stalks for health, attaching small framed mirrors to the ceiling above a candle chandelier, and building a custom fish tank stand for the homeowner's aquarium.

E6: Providence, RI: Wallis Avenue
Cast: Paige, Frank, Genevieve, Amy Wynn
Gen brings a touch of Tuscany to a bedroom by painting the walls sage green, painting the ceiling yellow, installing

floor-to-ceiling shelves, hanging ivy above the headboard, and using light and airy curtains and bed linens. Frank enlivens a kitchen by using several pastel shades of paint, creating a larger tabletop, laying a vinyl floor, and adding painted chevrons to the cabinets.

E7: Boston, MA: Ashfield Street

Cast: Paige, Genevieve, Laurie, Ty

Laurie breathes new life into a bedroom shared by two sisters by painting the walls lavender, creating a trundle bed, painting the existing furniture white, and using ribbons as accents. Gen adds a Moroccan touch to a girl's room by painting the walls and ceiling deep blue, installing a large curtained bed, hanging a Moroccan metal lamp, using gold fabric accents, and hanging white draperies.

E8: Springfield, MA: Sunset Terrace

Cast: Paige, Hildi, Vern, Ty

Hildi creates a Victorian look in a living room by painting the walls light taupe, using blue and white print fabric for draperies and slipcovers, painting blue stripes on the wood floor, sewing a white faux-fur rug, and transforming the fireplace with a custom-built Victorian-style mantelpiece. Vern goes for an even more Victorian look in the other living room by painting the walls yellow to highlight the homeowners' French Provençal furniture, laying a Victorian rug, making a light fixture with silver mesh and hand-strung beads, and creating a custom art piece using celestial and fleur-de-lis stencils.

E9: Boston, MA: Institute Road

Cast: Paige, Doug, Frank, Ty

Doug looks to the leaves for inspiration in his "Autumnal Bliss" bedroom. He papers the walls with bark paper, upholsters the headboard in linen, hangs yellow linen draperies, and frames fall leaves as art. Frank creates a Shakespearean library by painting the walls red, hand painting Elizabethan musician cutouts for the walls, and painting a rounded-stone pattern on the floor.

Vern's Room
Fairview Avenue, Chicago, IL

E10: Philadelphia, PA: Jeannes Street

Cast: Paige, Genevieve, Vern, Amy Wynn

Gen turns a basement den into a 3-D Scrabble board by painting taupe and white grids on the floors and ceiling, installing a black wall-length bar, making pillows that mimic Scrabble board squares, and framing game boards to hang on the wall. Vern uses the female homeowner's love of the holiday season for inspiration in a living room by painting the walls and ceiling deep red, making camel slipcovers and draperies, and building a dark wood armoire with mirrored doors.

E11: New Jersey: Perth Road

Cast: Paige, Frank, Laurie, Amy Wynn

Frank gives a living room a homier feel by adding light camel paint, a coffee table topped with a picture frame, textured folk art on the wall, and a custom-built armoire ("It's kind of a puppet theater cathedral"). Laurie redoes a bedroom without altering the existing Queen Anne furniture. She paints the walls a warm apricot, builds a custom canopy that rests on top of the four-poster bed, and adds bookshelves as nightstands.

E12: Maryland: Village Green

Cast: Paige, Doug, Genevieve, Amy Wynn

Gen refines a bedroom by painting one wall chocolate brown, covering the ceiling with gold metallic paint, installing a custom geometric shelving unit, making a fountain, decoupaging sewing patterns to a wall, and creating a light fixture out of a large wicker ball. Doug creates an elegant and sophisticated "Strip Stripe" look in a bedroom by painting the walls gray, building a large upholstered headboard with storage in the back, painting the furniture white, and painting large Matisse-inspired figures directly on the wall.

E13: Maryland: Fairway Court

Cast: Paige, Doug, Vern, Amy Wynn

Vern softens a bedroom by painting the walls a light gray, hanging charcoal draperies, suspending a canopy over the existing sleigh bed, and dangling 100 clear crystals from the canopy edge. Doug designs a fantasy bedroom suite for train enthusiasts by rounding the ceiling edges, covering the walls with blue paint and fabric, and building fake walls and windows to mimic the inside of a Pullman car.

E14: Chicago, IL: Edward Road

Cast: Paige, Frank, Laurie, Ty

Frank adds an aged-copper look to a kitchen by using touches of terra-cotta, copper, and green paint. He also lays earth-tone vinyl flooring, paints a faux-tile backsplash, makes a large floorcloth, and adds a butcher-block island. Laurie gives a living room a touch of European flair by painting a faux-fresco finish in yellow tones, installing dark wooden beams on the ceiling, hanging burlap draperies, painting a faux-inlay top on an occasional table, and repeating an X motif throughout the room.

E15: Chicago, IL: Spaulding Avenue

Cast: Paige, Doug, Hildi, Ty

Doug adds a little funk to a living room by painting the walls yellow, using Venetian plaster to make black and yellow blocks on a wall, upholstering the furniture with zebra-print fabric, and suspending a tabletop from the ceiling to create a dining area. Hildi brings the outdoors into a bedroom. She paints the walls cream and the trim a deep plum and then draws large "swooshes" of grass on the walls with chalk pastels. She adds a row of grass planter boxes along one wall, uses bursts of orange in pillows, and installs a large wooden bed.

E16: Chicago, IL: Fairview Avenue

Cast: Paige, Genevieve, Vern, Ty

Vern brightens a kitchen by painting the walls pear green, painting the cabinets white, creating a new cabinet for storage, making a new table, laying a black and white geometric rug, upholstering a storage bench that doubles as seating at the table, and hanging upholstered cushions against the wall above the bench. Gen gives the lodge look to a basement living room by painting the walls cinnamon, installing a pine plank ceiling, hanging wood wainscoting, slipcovering the furniture, and highlighting the fireplace with built-in shelves.

E17: Colorado: Berry Avenue

Cast: Paige, Genevieve, Hildi, Amy Wynn

Gen paints the walls of a kitchen bright eggplant, paints the cabinets vanilla-sage, removes the center panels of the cabinet doors to showcase the dishes inside, and prints each family member's face on a chair cover for personalized seating. Hildi creates an intimate living room by painting the walls a deep chocolate brown, using sage fabrics, transforming the coffee table into a large ottoman, and installing a wall-size fountain made to mimic the shape of the existing windows.

E18: Colorado: Cherry Street

Cast: Paige, Genevieve, Laurie, Amy Wynn

Gen gives a living room a punch of personality by painting the walls brick red with sage accents, hanging antlers on the walls, installing floor-to-ceiling shelving, making a focal point out of one of the homeowners' landscape photos, and creating an inlaid rug. Laurie applies a touch of mod to a living room by painting gray and yellow horizontal stripes on the walls, building a new glass-top coffee table, hanging silver silk draperies, and adding a piece of custom artwork.

E19: Colorado: Andes Way

Cast: Paige, Frank, Vern, Amy Wynn

Frank creates a family-friendly living room by rag-rolling the walls with cream and peach paint, hanging valances coated with brown builder's paper, building a white and sage armoire, and creating a kids' nook with a large art table, plant murals on the walls, and wooden clouds nailed to the ceiling. Vern stripes a living room, laying two colors of laminate flooring in alternating stripes, painting a red horizontal stripe on the khaki walls, and continuing the same stripe across the draperies.

E20: Colorado: Stoneflower Drive
Cast: Paige, Doug, Frank, Amy Wynn
Frank injects some whimsy into a bedroom by painting the walls celadon green, building a large headboard that mimics a skyline, creating a matching dog bed, and hanging gold curtains. Doug updates a living room with a design he calls "Smoke Screen." He paints the walls moss green, removes colonial molding, adds pewter accents, hangs pleated metal screening, and builds screen doors to cover shelving around the fireplace.

E21: Seattle, WA: 137th Street
Cast: Paige, Doug, Frank, Ty
Doug does "Denim Deluxe" in a living room. He paints a white grid pattern on chocolate walls, slipcovers the furniture with brown and ivory denim, makes art pieces with brightly colored tissue paper, lowers the existing coffee table, installs white wainscoting, and builds a white facade to cover the brick fireplace. Frank brightens a living room by painting the walls reddish orange and yellow, installing a new mantel, hanging shelves on either side of the fireplace, making a fireplace screen painted with folk art characters, and creating a window valance with place mats and clothespins.

E22: Seattle, WA: Dakota Street
Cast: Paige, Laurie, Vern, Ty
Vern adds drama and romance to a living room by painting the walls golden yellow, hanging brown draperies, building an armoire with red upholstered door panels, slipcovering the furniture in white fabric dyed with tea bags, and constructing red candle torchères. Laurie tries to convince her homeowners that she can warm up a bedroom with parchment-color paint, soft white and blue fabrics, various chocolate brown accents on the furniture and headboard, and painted partition screens.

E23: Seattle, WA: 56th Place
Cast: Paige, Genevieve, Hildi, Ty
Hildi entirely covers a basement rec room in magenta and taupe fabric hung from the ceiling. She also builds new coffee and side tables and slipcovers new sofas with magenta fabric. Gen creates an Asian living room, using shimmery silver and red paints and coating one wall in a metal paint that oxidizes to a rusted finish. She makes a valance out of an obi and uses cedar flowerpots as picture frames.

E24: Oregon: Alyssum Avenue
Cast: Paige, Genevieve, Hildi, Amy Wynn
Hildi creates a cozy bedroom by upholstering the walls and ceiling with silver-blue fabric, building a bed from storage cubes, draping sheer white fabric from the ceiling center over the bed corners, hanging a chandelier above

Doug's Room
137th Street, Seattle, WA

the bed, and adding a blue monogram to white bed linens. Gen adds a graphic touch to a living room by painting the walls bright yellow, covering a wall with 6-inch wooden squares, building cedar shelving under the stairs, and hanging clotheslines to display art and photos.

E25: Oregon: Alsea Court
Cast: Paige, Frank, Laurie, Amy Wynn
Frank goes south of the border in a kitchen by painting a serape on the ceiling, making a basket-weave wall treatment with sheet metal strips, painting the cabinet door center panels silver, designing a distressed tabletop, and upholstering dining chairs with serape fabric. Laurie brings warmth to a living room by painting the walls amber, using several expensive fabrics in warm harvest shades, building a long armoire with gold filigree door insets, and designing a large central ottoman.

E26: Portland, OR: Everett Street
Cast: Paige, Doug, Vern, Amy Wynn
Doug transforms a family room into an Art Deco theater by painting the floors and ceiling chocolate brown, covering the walls with chocolate brown fabric, building graduated platforms for silver chairs, suspending the television from the ceiling, and installing aisle lights. Vern creates a cohesive look in a living/dining room by painting the walls sage green and hanging sage draperies with white satin stripes on the windows and the walls of the dining area. He also builds a custom armoire and buffet with square wooden insets stained various colors and creates a custom lampshade with handmade art paper.

E27: Santa Clara, CA: Lafayette Street
Cast: Paige, Frank, Laurie, Ty
Frank adds a festive touch to the living room of a Delta Gamma residence by painting the walls two shades of a peachy orange; highlighting the curved ceiling with stenciled stars, triangles, swirls, and dots; painting the sorority letters above the fireplace; and installing a window bench seat. Laurie updates the Delta Gamma chapter room by painting the walls a muted seafoam, stenciling yellow anchors on the walls, designing a coffee table with hidden additional seating, and making a candelabra out of a captain's wheel.

E28: California: Corte Rosa
Cast: Paige, Laurie, Vern, Ty
Vern gives a bedroom an exotic resort decor by painting the walls light chino, upholstering the bedside tabletops with faux leather, adding tribal- and safari-print fabrics to the draperies and bed linens, hanging a red glass light fixture, and building storage cabinets on a large plant ledge. Laurie creates romance in a bedroom by painting the walls sage green, hanging a French tester canopy above the bed, painting the existing furniture mocha brown, installing a window seat with storage cabinets, and hanging dark green draperies.

E29: California: Grenadine Way
Cast: Paige, Frank, Vern, Ty
Vern looks to vintage Indian fabrics for inspiration in a bedroom. He paints the walls soft blue, lays wood laminate flooring, installs a large headboard of basket-woven iridescent fabric, and hangs amber glass candleholders. Frank gives ethnic flair to a living room by painting a mantel with stripes of mustard, white, taupe, and black; designing a large wooden sculpture; and building a new coffee table, armoire, and cornice box.

E30: Berkeley, CA: Prospect Street
Cast: Paige, Doug, Genevieve, Ty
Doug cleans up the Delta Upsilon fraternity chapter room (and goes "DU-clectic") by painting the walls lime green, installing bench seating, constructing two huge circular ottomans upholstered with lime and orange fabrics, and suspending a tabletop from the ceiling. Gen adds classic Hollywood-style glamour to the Alpha Omicron Pi sorority chapter room by painting white and silver stripes on the walls, adding black and silver throw pillows, building a large armoire, and commissioning her team to trace silhouettes of Paige and herself for wall art.

E31: Oakland, CA: Webster Street
Cast: Paige, Genevieve, Hildi, Amy Wynn
Hildi covers the walls of a living room with straw. She also installs a wall of bookshelves, covers the fireplace with copper mesh and glass rods, applies pink textured plaster to the ceiling, and screens the windows with wooden louvered blinds. Gen brightens a kitchen by

painting the cabinets yellow and the walls cobalt blue, building a tile-top island and kids' table, personalizing dishware with family art and photos, and designing a backlit display shelf for a glass bottle collection.

E32: California: Peralta Street

Cast: Paige, Doug, Hildi, Amy Wynn

Hildi divides a living room into quadrants by painting two opposite corners of the room and ceiling silver and painting the remaining corners and ceiling space violet. She supplements the look with a clear-glass mosaic on the fireplace surround, four industrial-style chairs, and a large circular ottoman upholstered in silver and violet. Doug thinks pink in a dining room. He paints the walls bubble gum pink, paints the ceiling chocolate brown, hangs a lamp upside down from the ceiling, upholsters new white dining chairs with lime green T-shirts, and tops new storage units with green gazing balls.

E33: Los Angeles, CA: Willoughby Avenue

Cast: Paige, Doug, Genevieve, Ty

Doug sees red in a living room: He stencils the walls and doors in red and white, using a rectangular graphic based on an existing pillow pattern. He paints the ceiling gray, lays a red shag rug, and builds a U-shape couch with red upholstery. Gen designs a swingin' living room with 1950s flair by painting the walls aqua, disguising stains on the wood floor by painting it black, transforming mod place mats into wall sconces, slipcovering a futon in white vinyl, and laying a bookcase on its side to create a new coffee table.

E34: Los Angeles, CA: Springdale Drive

Cast: Paige, Laurie, Vern, Ty

Vern brightens a dining room by painting the walls yellow, hanging bronze draperies, installing a wall-length buffet with built-in storage, and designing a multiarmed halogen chandelier with gold vellum shades and a hanging candleholder. Laurie enlivens a basement den by painting the walls yellow, slipcovering the existing furniture with natural cotton duck fabric, sewing an aqua Roman shade,

installing several yellow and aqua shadow box shelves, designing a folding screen to mask exercise equipment, and painting squares and rectangles in various shades of aqua to create custom wall art.

E35: California: Abbeywood Lane

Cast: Paige, Frank, Hildi, Ty

Frank gives a living room a cohesive look by painting the walls sage green; building an upholstered wall hanging in shades of peach, coral, and yellow; painting a life-size image of the homeowners' toddler on the wall; making throw pillows out of fabric designed by the homeowner; and crafting candleholders out of 4x4s covered with license plates. Hildi creates her version of a nautical living room by painting the walls black, nailing 120 lightly stained 1x2s on the walls in a vertical arrangement about 2 inches apart, building two large mirror-image couches upholstered in seafoam fabric, creating seafoam throw pillows and draperies, and mounting photos of the ocean onto blocks of wood.

E36: Austin, TX: La Costa Drive (Celebrity Episode)

Cast: Paige, Hildi, Vern, Ty

In the first celebrity episode of *Trading Spaces*, Vern breathes life into the bonus room of Dixie Chicks lead vocalist Natalie Maines. Vern paints the walls yellow; installs a wall-length desk and sewing unit; hangs a huge chandelier; and sews throw pillows, draperies, and bed linens with shimmery red fabric. Hildi adds style to a sewing room, which belongs to Natalie's mother, by railroading gray and sage fabric on the walls, installing wooden louvered wall dividers, building a 14-foot-long couch, reupholstering a vintage shampoo chair with sage chenille, and covering a coffee table with slate tiles.

E37: Texas: Sherwood Street

Cast: Paige, Frank, Genevieve, Amy Wynn

Frank transforms a kitchen by removing strawberry-print wallpaper, sponge-painting a focal-point wall, hanging new draperies with a pear motif, painting faux tiles on the avocado green floor and countertops, and hanging a thin plywood sunburst around the existing fluorescent light. Gen conjures a New England cottage feel in a bedroom by painting three of the walls pale smoke-gray, painting one of the walls ultrabright white, building a fireplace mantel-style

after

L:aurie's Room
Rodney Bay, Wake Forest, NC

headboard, creating curtain tiebacks from red neckties, sewing bed pillows from pinstriped suit jackets, distressing the existing ceiling fan blades, and adding a reading nook.

E38: Houston, TX: Sawdust Street

Cast: Paige, Doug, Laurie, Amy Wynn

Laurie refines a living room by painting the walls margarine yellow, building a wall-length bookshelf, hanging bamboo blinds and yellow drapery panels, and adding two spicy orange chairs. Doug goes "Zen/Goth" in a living room by painting the walls blood red, building an L-shape couch, hanging a large wrought-iron light fixture, adding a black faux-fur rug, and enlarging a photo of the female homeowner in lingerie and knee-high boots to hang over the fireplace.

E39: Houston, TX: Appalachian Trail

Cast: Paige, Doug, Laurie, Amy Wynn

Laurie adds style to an office/playroom by painting the walls terra-cotta, building a large shelving and desk unit with plumbing conduit, painting the existing coffee table and armoire in cream and black, adding new seating, and creating the illusion of symmetry with cream draperies on an off-center window. Doug goes for a soft look in a bedroom by painting the walls pale blue, upholstering a tall headboard in blue chenille, sewing new blue and white bed linens, and installing custom light fixtures. He titles the room "A Pretty Room by Doug."

E40: Plano, TX: Bent Horn Court

Cast: Paige, Genevieve, Vern, Ty

Gen gets in touch with her inner child as she designs a playroom, painting multicolor polka dots on the walls, cutting movable circles of green outdoor carpeting for the floors, building a large castle-shape puppet theater, hanging fabric-covered tire swings, and designing four upholstered squares on wheels with storage space inside. Vern gets in touch with his rustic side in a living room by laying natural-color adhesive carpet tiles, painting an existing armoire and other furniture pieces black, and building a combination ottoman/coffee table/bench unit.

after

Hildi's Room
Peralta Street, California

Laurie's Room
Sawdust Street, Houston, TX

after

E41: Plano, TX: Shady Valley Road

Cast: Paige, Doug, Hildi, Ty

Hildi creates a two-tone bedroom by painting the walls bright white, installing 12-inch orange baseboards, building new head- and footboards that match the pitch of the cathedral ceiling and slipcovering them in white, and upholstering a chair with white faux fur. Doug adds sophisticated style to a playroom by painting the wall moss green ("Moss Madness"), installing beams on the ceiling in a barnlike formation, building a basket-weave armoire, revamping a futon into a daybed, and hanging bifold doors on a toy closet.

E42: Texas: Sutton Court

Cast: Paige, Frank, Laurie, Ty

Laurie designs a kitchen, using the homeowners' china for inspiration. She paints the walls taupe with white trim, builds large wooden shadow boxes to display china pieces, hangs new light fixtures, and uses taupe fabric for the window treatments and chair cushions. Frank works with a Southwest theme in a living room, adding chamois-cloth accents to the existing furniture, building a footstool out of a saddle, hanging several custom-made art pieces, designing a Mission-style armoire, and making potted "cactus" out of vegetables.

E43: Raleigh, NC: Legging Lane

Cast: Paige, Frank, Hildi, Amy Wynn

Hildi adds romance to a bedroom by painting the walls slate gray, hanging smoky plum draperies, sewing a tufted lavender coverlet, framing a favorite picture of the Eiffel Tower, and building cubic bench seats and nightstands. Frank lets his creativity flow in a playroom by painting the walls, furniture, doors, and floors in a multitude of pastel colors. He also hides a large refrigerator, builds an armoire to house media equipment, and designs a large toy chest.

E44: North Carolina: Southerby Drive

Cast: Paige, Doug, Hildi, Amy Wynn

Doug adds an Eastern touch to a bedroom by painting the walls china blue and painting white chinoiserie murals. He builds a black four-poster bed with PVC pipe, adds a custom-built sculpture, hangs white draperies, and paints the furniture black. He aptly titles his room "China Blue." Hildi also displays Eastern influences in a bedroom, painting the walls a soft green and installing a wall of shoji screens to create a headboard. She covers the screens and the existing furniture with a lavender crackle finish, hangs lavender draperies, and upholsters a sofa with purple fabric.

E45: Wake Forest, NC: Rodney Bay

Cast: Paige, Laurie, Vern, Amy Wynn

Vern adds drama to a bedroom by painting the walls gray, attaching a fabric canopy to the ceiling, designing a headboard with interior lights that shine out of the top, painting the existing furniture black, and upholstering a chair with gray flannel. Laurie brightens a living room by painting the walls a bold shade of green, installing two floor-to-ceiling shelving units with crown molding, hanging yellow draperies, adding several pillows in warm harvest shades to the existing off-white sofa, and hanging a new parchment-shade light fixture.

Season 3....

E1: Maine: George Road

Cast: Paige, Doug, Genevieve, Ty

Doug adds warmth to a kitchen by painting the walls umber, painting the woodwork white, installing a butcher-block countertop, building a large pantry unit with bifold doors, and sewing a large tablecloth. Gen updates a dark kitchen by painting the walls bright green, installing a black and white tile countertop, building a butcher-block island, hanging wood laminate wall paneling, and installing a 1930s-style light fixture.

E2: Portland, OR: Rosemont Avenue

Cast: Paige, Laurie, Vern, Ty

Laurie goes nautical in a living room by painting the walls deep aqua blue, painting the fireplace white, putting a cream-tone paint wash on wooden chairs and upholstering them with zebra-print fabric, and installing a vintage mercury glass chandelier. Vern brightens a living room by painting the walls yellow, hanging black and yellow Roman shades, installing French doors, covering the ceiling with white steel squares, hanging a ceiling fan, using black slipcovers for the existing furniture, and adding silver fold-up trays to serve as side tables and a coffee table.

E3: Maine: Joseph Drive

Cast: Paige, Frank, Laurie, Ty

Laurie enlivens a bedroom by painting the walls soft yellow, building an Asian-style shelving unit, designing a new headboard, sewing gray and white toile bedding, and adding an unusual floral light fixture. Frank shows another side of his design style in a bachelor's bedroom: He paints the walls and ceiling dark blue-green, hangs simple white draperies, sews a large plastic envelope to hold a pencil drawing of a leaf on the wall, builds a table that houses three wooden bins, and adds pet collars to a rocking chair.

E4: Long Island, NY: Steuben Boulevard

Cast: Paige, Edward, Frank, Ty

Edward jazzes up a bedroom by painting the walls light mocha, hanging wall sconces, building an Art Deco armoire, painting Deco patterns on the closet doors, installing lights around the bottom edge of the bed frame, hanging a canopy, and painting a faux-malachite finish on the furniture tops and wall sconces. Frank gets woodsy in a dining room, painting the walls deep orange, installing pine doors between the dining room and kitchen, creating a coffee table out of a large flowerpot, painting white birch trees all around the room, and making a large pig-topped weather vane to sit above the fireplace.

E5: Long Island, NY: Split Rock Road

Cast: Paige, Genevieve, Vern, Amy Wynn

Gen brightens a dark kitchen by painting the walls white, the trim celadon green, the window shutters pale blue, and the cabinets yellow. She also polishes the existing copper stove hood, hangs white wooden slats on one wall, builds a butcher-block table, skirts the dining chairs in white fabric, and coats a new light fixture with copper spray paint. Her design is inspired by a sea-glass necklace the homeowner wears nearly every day. Vern adds a soft touch to a kitchen by painting the walls and cabinet door insets green, painting parts of the cabinet doors white, stenciling white fleurs-de-lis on the cabinet doors, building a new laminate countertop, laying a two-tone parquet floor, using green toile fabrics on Roman shades and table linens, adding touches of green gingham to the tablecloth, and adding several green-shaded table lamps to the countertop.

E6: New York: Whitlock Road

Cast: Paige, Doug, Genevieve, Amy Wynn

Gen designs a bedroom with an espresso color scheme: She paints the walls café au lait, uses darker java on the ceiling beams, and paints sections of the ceiling cream. She also sews orange asterisks on a white bedspread, builds a combination headboard/desk, and exposes original wood flooring. Doug updates a bedroom by painting squares on the wall in multiple shades of sage, building a mantel-like headboard, designing S-shape side tables, sewing stripes of yarn on a white bedspread, and framing strips of wood veneer for bedside art. He titles the room "Don't Box Me In."

E7: New York: Half Hollow Turn

Cast: Paige, Frank, Kia, Amy Wynn

Frank updates a living room by painting the walls bamboo yellow, adding black accents on the walls and the furniture, using concrete stepping-stones to create side tables, converting a garden bench into a coffee table, and hanging a custom sculpture made from electrical and plumbing components. Kia gets funky in a basement rec room by painting the walls purple and light green, building a wall-length bench with purple velvet upholstery, hanging a swirly purple wallpaper border, installing halogen lights on a running cable, and creating green draperies.

E8: Philadelphia, PA: 22nd Street

Cast: Paige, Edward, Genevieve, Ty

Edward adds ethnic flair to a living room by painting the walls red, texturing the fireplace with black paint and tissue paper, hanging an existing rug on the wall, building a chaise lounge with finial feet, and installing an entertainment center made of shadow boxes. Gen heads to Cuba in a bedroom by covering the walls with white textured paint, adding a faux-wood grain finish to the doors, building a headboard enhanced with a blown-up image from a Cuban cigar box, designing lighted plastic bed tables, and creating picture frames out of cigar boxes.

E9: Philadelphia, PA: Gettysburg Lane

Cast: Paige, Frank, Vern, Ty

Frank updates a kitchen by painting the walls and cabinets several different colors, laying a stone-look vinyl tile, installing a new countertop, adding decorative elements to a half-wall to create a new serving bar, and mounting plates with wooden food cutouts across the soffit. Vern adds his version of cottage style to a living room by painting the walls yellow, installing white wainscoting, building a 12-foot-wide shelving and storage unit, framing large copies of old family photos, making a "quilt" of images to hang above the storage unit, and adding touches of denim fabric throughout the room.

E10: Pennsylvania: Gorski Lane

Cast: Paige, Doug, Frank, Ty

Frank adds a celestial touch in a bedroom by painting the ceiling deep plum and painting silver stars across it. He paints the walls with several shades of cream and green, adds small blocks of color to the paneled doors, builds a writing desk, hangs a small cabinet upside down on the wall, installs a ceiling fan, and makes several pieces of custom artwork. Doug brings some "jungle boogie" to a bedroom by painting zebra stripes across all four walls, painting the ceiling dark brown, suspending a bamboo grid from the ceiling, building a breakfast table and chairs from scavenged lumber, and covering the existing headboard with sticks and bamboo.

E11: Long Island, NY: Dover Court

Cast: Paige, Edward, Vern, Amy Wynn

Vern sets a boy's bedroom in motion by painting the walls various shades of blue, building a race car bed with working headlights, suspending a working train track and toy planes from the ceiling, hanging a motorcycle swing made from recycled tires, and hanging precut letters on the walls to spell out words like "woosh" and "zoom." Edward brings the outdoors into a bedroom by painting the walls moss green and antiquing a landscape print above the bed. He alters prefab side tables with filigreelike cuts, disguises the existing lamps with black spray paint and fabric slipcovers, hangs antique glass shutters over the windows, and builds a large entertainment center using the existing side tables and more glass shutters.

E12: Pennsylvania: Victoria Drive

Cast: Paige, Doug, Kia, Amy Wynn

Doug creates a cabin feel in a living room by covering

the walls in soft brown-tinted Venetian plaster, hanging red Roman shades, covering a ready-made coffee table with leather, staining the existing sofa and coffee tables a darker color, sewing cow-print throw pillows, building a large armoire covered with rough-cut poplar, and hanging leftover lumber on the walls in decorative stripes. Kia creates her version of an indoor garden in a guest bedroom by painting the walls yellow, hanging a flowery wallpaper border on the ceiling, creating a duvet from synthetic turf and silk flowers, building a headboard from a tree limb, hanging a chair swing from a cedar arbor, placing gravel under the swing, and building a picket fence room divider.

E13: New Jersey: Manitoba Trail

Cast: Paige, Doug, Frank, Amy Wynn

Frank goes all out in a country living/dining room by painting the walls light green, distressing the wood floors, painting a faux rug beneath the coffee table, applying several decorative paint colors and finishes to an antique cabinet, building custom lamps with large antique yarn spools, and creating three homemade country-girl dolls with pillow forms. Doug brightens a living room by painting everything—the walls, ceiling, ceiling beams, fireplace, and ceiling fans—bright white ("White Whoa"). He buys two new white sofas, hangs bright blue draperies, installs a new doorbell that blends into the white wall, sews many brightly colored throw pillows, makes a large framed mirror, and creates custom art pieces.

E14: Nazareth, PA: First Street

Cast: Paige, Doug, Vern, Amy Wynn

Vern adds a touch of serenity to a living room by painting three walls taupe and one wall deep blue, adding a new mantel, sewing throw pillows with a wave-motif fabric, suspending mini symbiotic environments from the ceiling, building a coffee table with a center inset of sand and candles, and placing six fountains around the fireplace. Doug gives a kitchen an earthy feel by laying brown peel-and-stick vinyl flooring, painting the walls beige, installing new orange laminate countertops, painting the cabinets yellow with an orange glaze, adding crown molding to the cabinet tops, building a pie safe, and upholstering the dining chairs with red-orange fabric.

E15: New Jersey: Catania Court

Cast: Paige, Genevieve, Hildi, Amy Wynn

Hildi has the golden touch in a bedroom: She paints the walls yellow-green, sews bedding with fabrics she purchased in India, uses batik-inspired stamps to create gold accents on the ceiling and around the room, replaces the existing baseboards with taller ones, adds a gold wash to the existing furniture, builds a low-slung "opium couch," and hangs a vintage glass light fixture. Gen finds the silver lining in a dining room: She paints the walls orange-red, hangs silver crown molding, paints the trim and chair rail ivory, hangs ivory and silver draperies, paints

Vern's Room
First Street, Nazareth, PA

`01:39:32.08`
after

`01:40:15.20.2`
after

Edward's Room
Dover Court, Long Island, NY

a canvas floorcloth to lay under the table, and hangs a new light fixture that has small tree limbs attached to it

E16: Philadelphia, PA: East Avenue

Cast: Paige, Frank, Hildi, Amy Wynn

Hildi gets graphic in a living room by painting three walls yellow, covering one wall with a large Lichtenstein-inspired portrait of herself, adding a glass-shelf bar area, building all new tables and chairs, sewing cushions with mod pink and orange fabric, and re-covering a thrift store couch with red fabric. Frank brightens a living room by painting the walls deep purple, painting the ceiling bright red, designing a coffee table unit with four bases that move apart and become extra seating, and creating wall art with rain gutter materials and round wooden cutouts.

E17: Virginia: Gentle Heights Court

Cast: Paige, Hildi, Kia, Ty

Hildi sets up camp in a boy's bedroom by painting the walls and ceiling midnight blue, hanging a moon-shape light fixture, placing glow-in-the-dark stars on the ceiling, hanging a solar system mobile, building a 13-foot-tall rock climbing wall, adding several pieces of fold-up camping furniture, placing the mattress in a room-size tent, using a blue sleeping bag as a duvet, and placing camping lanterns around the room. Kia adds sensuous details to a bedroom by painting the walls orange and the trim Grecian blue, hanging a red and gold wallpaper border, creating a Taj Mahal cutout to place around the existing entertainment center, installing two wooden columns from India, adding bedding made from sari fabrics, and suspending the bed from the ceiling with chains.

E18: Arlington, VA: First Road

Cast: Paige, Doug, Hildi, Ty

Hildi gift-wraps a bedroom by painting the walls Tiffany-box aqua blue, adding a duvet and Roman shades in the same aqua blue, airbrushing white "ribbons" on the walls and fabrics, hanging white lamps with square shades above the headboard, building acrylic side tables that light up from inside, and adding bright silver accents. Doug warms up a bedroom by painting the walls and ceiling a deep gray-blue; hanging white Roman shades, brown silk curtains, and cornice boards; constructing a headboard from a large existing window frame; balancing the headboard with a new armoire that features white silk door insets; and creating custom artwork in brown and navy. He titles the room "Framed."

E19: Washington, D.C.: Quebec Place

Cast: Paige, Genevieve, Vern, Ty

Gen dishes up a serene living room inspired by her favorite Thai soup. She paints the walls a light bone color and gives the room lemongrass green accents, a newly constructed sofa, a wall-length valance with lemongrass curtains, and lotus flower light fixtures. Vern turns up the heat in a newlywed couple's bedroom by painting the fireplace and dressing room red, installing a floor-to-ceiling mirrored wall in the dressing area, hanging rows of crystals above the fireplace, sewing red silk Roman shades, and installing a large headboard with red silk insets.

E20: Indiana: River Valley Drive

Cast: Paige, Doug, Genevieve, Amy Wynn

Gen tones down a brightly colored living room by painting the walls a sleek silver-gray, painting the existing furniture white, designing a new entertainment center made out of stacked white boxes with punched-aluminum door insets, and adding a few bold touches of color with green curtains, a new green room screen, and a fuchsia ottoman. Doug puts his foot down in his "Back from Brazil" living room, hanging a three-section painting of his own foot. He also stencils white flowers—inspired by sarongs—on the walls, slipcovers the existing furniture in white, highlights the fireplace mantel with a large vertical wooden extension, designs an acrylic light fixture, and sews throw pillows from tie-dyed sarongs.

E21: Indiana: Fieldhurst Lane

Cast: Paige, Doug, Vern, Amy Wynn

Doug gets back to his Midwestern roots in a bedroom by painting the walls orange, installing wainscoting upholstered with tan fabric, creating custom paintings of wheat and corn, embellishing simple white bedding with orange ribbon and yarn, and designing a large armoire. Vern sets a restful scene in a bedroom by painting the walls a light blue, attaching oak plywood squares to a wall, painting the existing furniture black, reupholstering a chaise lounge with dark blue velvet, hanging blue velvet draperies, wrapping the bed frame with white beaded garland, and installing new sconces and a ceiling fixture with white beaded shades.

E22: Indianapolis, IN: Halleck Way

Cast: Paige, Edward, Kia, Amy Wynn

Edward designs a soft yet masculine bedroom by painting the tray ceiling slate blue and white, painting the walls and existing furniture tan, hanging a customized light fixture with a hand-painted glass frame, draping white fabric across the length of one wall, hanging brown draperies made from lush fabrics, and slipcovering the head- and footboards. He also rearranges the furniture and creates neoclassic wall shelves. Kia walks like an Egyptian in a bedroom by painting the walls "Tut Wine" and "Pharaoh Gold," building pyramid-shape cornice boards, and hanging framed Egyptian prints and a handmade Eye of Horus. She also paints a personalized hieroglyphic message for the homeowners ("David loves Noel") on an existing room screen and installs a ceiling fan with palm leaves attached to the blades.

E23: Missouri: Sunburst Drive

Cast: Paige, Genevieve, Vern, Ty

Gen draws inspiration for a bedroom from gauchos

Vern's Room
Quebec Place, Washington, D.C.

Gen's Room
River Valley Drive, Indiana

(Argentino cowboys): She paints the walls deep brown, creates faux crown molding by bringing the ceiling paint several inches down onto the walls, installs a woven leather-and-red-velvet headboard, and glues pictures of gauchos to the closet doors. She also builds an upholstered bench and pulls in furniture from other rooms that matches the room's color scheme. Vern adds a masculine edge to a girlie bedroom by painting the walls soft blue, painting the existing furniture and doors red, designing a wall-length desk and computer hutch, installing a headboard made of upholstered leather squares, and adding several wrought-iron light fixtures and Moroccan-inspired accents.

E24: Scott Air Force Base, MO: Ash Creek

Cast: Paige, Doug, Kia, Ty

Doug travels down Route 66 in a child's bedroom by laying gray carpet, painting highway stripes and road signs on the walls, and installing a front and back end from two actual cars. (He adds a mattress in the back end of one car, and the front end of the other car serves as a toy chest.) Kia creates "Military Chic" in a living/dining room, using various shades of gray paint, new chair rails, a gray and white camouflage wallpaper border, pillows and cushions in the same camouflage color combination, a new storage bench, a faux fireplace, a red slipcover, red decorative accents, and draperies made from a gray parachute.

E25: Missouri: Sweetbriar Lane

Cast: Paige, Edward, Frank, Ty

Edward designs a sleek bedroom by painting the walls shades of gray, white, and China blue; adding extra closet and storage space; and designing a mirrored entertainment armoire to conceal the TV. He also hangs a light fixture wrapped in pearls; adds gray, purple, blue, and green fabrics; and creates a sculpture from curled metal. Frank creates an eclectic bedroom, painting the walls orange and installing large eyes made of copper tubing above the bed. An upholstered lip headboard completes the face, and a new platform bed stands beneath it. Frank paints the fireplace purple and creates an artistic theme by attaching a giant pencil on one wall and painting female figures near it to look as though they'd been sketched.

E26: London, England: Garden Flat

Cast: Paige, Genevieve, Hildi, Handy Andy

Gen enlivens a bedroom by painting the walls a rich, spicy orange, painting a small alcove red, and hanging many yellow-green draperies. She also builds a new platform bed with drawers beneath, adds a ready-made dresser, creates closet space along one wall, installs crown molding, and hangs rows of framed Chinese newsprint. Hildi brightens a bedroom shared by two girls by splattering brightly colored paint onto white walls, laying fluffy white carpet, framing the girls' artwork, and sewing rainbow-color draperies. She also installs doors on an existing wall-size shelving unit, builds beds and nightstands on casters, and creates a "secret garden" area with wheat grass plants.

E27: Mississippi: Golden Pond

Cast: Paige, Hildi, Laurie, Amy Wynn
Laurie updates a bedroom by painting the walls camel-yellow, building a large headboard of upholstered aqua fabric with a chocolate brown grid overlay, creating a large mirror from smaller mirrored squares, hanging a thrift store chandelier, adding new upholstered thrift store chairs, using aqua and camel-yellow bedding, and building new chocolate brown bookcases. Hildi adds color to a bathroom (a *Trading Spaces* first!) by stapling more than 6,000 silk flowers to the walls, painting the trim and cabinets gold, creating red acrylic cabinet door inserts, building a bench upholstered in terry cloth, and sewing draperies and a shower curtain from French floral fabrics.

after ◄

Gen's Room
Camino Mojada, San Clemente, CA

E28: Mississippi: Winsmere Way

Cast: Paige, Hildi, Laurie, Amy Wynn
Laurie spices up the bedroom of a newly divorced homeowner with cumin yellow paint on the walls, an eggplant-color ceiling, a large upholstered headboard with nailhead trim, a new chaise lounge, a blown-glass light fixture, and two upholstered message boards. Hildi adds drama to a bedroom by covering the walls in red toile fabric, painting the ceiling smoky plum, slipcovering a thrift store sofa with cream fabric, building a new armoire with curved doors, repainting two thrift store lamps, and creating shadow boxes.

E29: San Antonio, TX: Ghostbridge

Cast: Paige, Hildi, Vern, Ty
Hildi gets groovy in a living room by lining one wall with record albums and painting the remaining walls purple, yellow, teal, and orange. She creates slipcovers in the same colors, makes a coffee tabletop by covering a colorful scarf with a large piece of glass, paints the homeowners' favorite chair black with brightly colored flowers, installs lamps made from French drainpipes, and designs a large entertainment center. Vern leaves his mark in a living room by covering one wall with wood veneer wallpaper, bringing in new pieces of brown furniture, hanging red draperies, creating a red and gold leaf coffee table and room screen, and laying a red rug.

E30: Austin, TX: Wyoming Valley Drive

Cast: Paige, Hildi, Laurie, Ty
Laurie adds warmth to a dining room by weaving one wall with brown sueded cotton and painting the other walls pink-orange. She builds a round dining table with a stenciled top and a fabric skirt, designs a buffet table with legs made from plumbing conduit, and makes

draperies and seat cushions from green fabric. Hildi creates a sleek kitchen by covering the walls with peel-and-stick wine labels, painting the cabinets black, enlarging an existing bench, designing a large pot rack from lumber and copper plumbing conduit, painting the existing wooden blinds black and orange, slipcovering the dining chairs with orange fabric, and embellishing the dining table with gold accents.

E31: Austin, TX: Aire Libre Drive

Cast: Paige, Frank, Kia, Ty
Frank adds drama to a living room by painting one wall orange and the other walls yellow, building two new end tables, designing a massive coffee table out of a black granite slab and four decorative columns, adding a toy chest to hold dog toys, covering the existing furniture with multicolor fabric, and laying a new rug. Kia updates a living room by painting the walls moss green and brown, painting a golden glaze over the brown paint, designing new draperies from various types of printed fabric, building a large frame above the fireplace, adding a new love seat, and scavenging accessories from other rooms in the house.

E32: Austin, TX: Wampton Way

Cast: Paige, Doug, Genevieve, Ty
Gen adds an Art Deco touch to a living room by colorwashing the walls in various shades of yellow and orange, slipcovering the existing furniture with graphic black and white fabric, building up the existing fireplace with black and mahogany accents, suspending the television with cables and a wooden shelf, adding two large topiaries, and framing various champagne and liqueur posters. Doug gives a living room an antique

Spanish flair by building a large dark brown fireplace facade, painting the walls smoky green, and staining the existing barstools a darker brown. He adds a chair upholstered in newspaper-print fabric and creates wall art with canvas and newspapers.

E33: San Clemente, CA: Camino Mojada

Cast: Paige, Genevieve, Vern, Ty
Gen adds Polynesian flair to a bedroom by building a grass-cloth headboard, hanging mosquito netting, painting the walls smoky taupe, painting the existing furniture orange, sewing two new dog beds from the same material as the new bedspread, planting several large palm plants, and building a large square shelving unit to hold accessories and a TV. Vern cozies up a loft TV room by attaching several upholstered diamond shapes on two walls, building new black velvet upholstered sofas, designing a large black coffee table with upholstered panels, framing photocopies of Hollywood movie legends on vellum, installing new shelving to hold entertainment equipment, and hanging several black and taupe drapery panels to close off the room.

E34: California: Dusty Trail

Cast: Paige, Doug, Genevieve, Ty
Doug designs a bedroom he calls "Cosmo Shab" by colorwashing the walls with three shades of blue paint, painting the cathedral ceiling gray, installing crown molding, hanging a chandelier removed from the dining room, sewing gray and white toile draperies, painting the existing furniture white, and distressing the newly painted pieces to create an antique look. Gen transforms a kitchen into a French *boucherie* (butcher shop) by covering the walls with green chalkboard paint, painting

the cabinets vanilla with gray insets, installing a tin ceiling, building a larger tabletop, and hanging pictures of "meat puppets" around the room.

E35: California: Fairfield
Cast: Paige, Frank, Kia, Ty
Kia updates an office/game room by painting the walls apricot and the trim orange. She builds a love seat that sits 8 inches off the ground, designs a removable tabletop for an existing game table, builds storage cubes that double as seats, hangs a "mirror" made of CDs, makes chess pieces from copper pipe, and rearranges the existing desk to create a more effective office area. Frank designs a "tranquil love nest" in a bedroom, adding coffee-color paint, a new coffee bar (complete with a small refrigerator), wooden chevrons on the existing furniture, gauzy fabric draped around the four-poster bed, and a large piece of bamboo for a drapery rod.

E36: San Diego, CA: Duenda Road
Cast: Paige, Frank, Vern, Amy Wynn
Frank adds romance to a bedroom by painting the walls soft green, building a canopy frame from molding strips, hanging a gauzy canopy from the ceiling, and revamping an existing dresser. Vern updates a living room by painting the walls with two tones of soft green, surrounding the existing fireplace with slate tiles, painting the existing furniture a third shade of green, hanging glass vases on the wall, installing green chenille draperies, and creating a new entertainment center.

E37: Los Angeles, CA: Murietta Avenue
Cast: Paige, Genevieve, Laurie, Amy Wynn
Gen gives a bland living/dining room a 1940s L.A. twist by painting the walls dark red, painting the trim bright white, adding white crown molding, and hanging draperies featuring a palm frond print. Gen also designs lighted display shelves, frames book illustrations of L.A. in the 1940s, reupholsters the dining room chairs with more palm frond fabrics, and hangs a new period light fixture. Laurie creates a warm and comfortable living room by

painting the walls butter yellow, with bands of golden camel and cream near the top of the walls. She installs built-in wall cabinets to house electronic equipment and "hideaway dog beds," lays a large khaki area rug, paints the fireplace white, slipcovers the sofa, and adds two green chenille chairs.

E38: Scottsdale, AZ: Dell Road
Cast: Paige, Frank, Vern, Ty
Frank adds a touch of whimsy to a girl's bedroom by painting geometric shapes on the walls with different shades of pastel paints; painting different sections of the walls purple; installing a desk unit that looks like a monkey; laying a multicolor rug; designing a doll-inspired TV cabinet; and adding blue beanbag chairs, multicolored linens, and large throw pillows. Vern creates a soothingly sexy bedroom by painting two walls deep purple, covering two walls and the ceiling with maple planks, building a birch platform bed, installing a cable lighting fixture, hanging mirrored candle sconces throughout the room, designing a long entertainment/storage bench, and re-covering an existing sofa with dark purple fabric.

E39: Scottsdale, AZ: Windrose Avenue
Cast: Paige, Doug, Frank, Ty
Doug transforms a large bedroom into two intimate areas by building a large I-shape wall in the center of the room: He places the existing bed on one side of the wall and places a sofa and armoire removed from other rooms in the house on the other side of the wall. He also paints the walls yellow and the new wall rust-red, sews new rust and yellow bedding with mod square embellishments, designs a plank-style coffee table, and hangs two of the homeowners' favorite tulip paintings on each side of the wall. He titles the room "Barrier." Frank transports a bedroom to India during the colonial period by painting the walls deep purple, reusing the existing navy drapes, adding a navy valance with gold stenciling, creating nightstands from inverted bamboo trash cans, adding lamps with beaded shades, and converting an existing dresser into a TV armoire.

E40: Vegas, NV: Carlsbad Caverns
Cast: Paige, Doug, Hildi, Amy Wynn
To redecorate a living room, Hildi draws inspiration from a print she bought in London. She paints the walls dark red; paints the ceiling blue; adds six red columns throughout the room; lays checkerboard vinyl flooring in two shades of orange; hangs deep red draperies; and adds slipcovers, upholstery, and pillows in every shade of the rainbow. Doug gets "Dirty" in a bedroom by covering the walls in dark brown Venetian plaster. He paints the ceiling peach, hangs bright blue draperies, sews pillows and bedding in various blue fabrics, installs crown molding, builds a large round white armoire, and creates a four-poster look around the existing bed with four alleged stripper poles.

E41: Vegas, NV: Smokemont Courts
Cast: Paige, Edward, Laurie, Amy Wynn
Edward designs a hip, funky office with one purple wall. He paints the remaining walls and ceiling light gray, constructs a large black built-in desk, designs black shelving, uses the homeowner's guitars as artwork, creates window shades from plastic sheets and paper clips, drapes white fabric across one wall, and incorporates a gray flannel chaise lounge. Laurie updates a bland living room by painting the walls taupe, building a large square shelving unit, painting the shelving insets coral, laying a large brown area rug, hanging conduit piping as drapery rods, hanging a piece of fabric as artwork, utilizing the existing black love seats, adding a square coffee table, and converting an existing side table into an ottoman.

E42: Vegas, NV: Woodmore Court
Cast: Paige, Genevieve, Vern, Amy Wynn
Gen goes bold in a living room by painting plant ledges in various shades of purple, building a dark wooden surround for the fireplace and TV cabinet, hanging two raspberry-shape light fixtures, painting a stained-glass treatment on the windows, designing a square coffee table with an inset basket center filled with floating candles, and hanging long white linen curtains. Vern re-creates the feel of a breezy summer day in a living room by painting light yellow 1-foot-wide stripes across the walls, building a large white armoire, adding doors that match the armoire to an existing wall niche, slipcovering the existing furniture with blue fabric, transforming two thrift store computer desks into a square coffee table, and installing white crown molding.

E43: Miami, FL: Ten Court
Cast: Paige, Hildi, Kia, Ty
Hildi adds an art gallery look to a living room with periwinkle blue walls, a slipcovered thrift store sofa to match the walls, a new brick paver floor, a wooden slat bench-style coffee table, track lighting, and canvases covered in several pastel paints blended into one another. Kia heads toward

after

Kia's Room
Fairfield, California

Frank's Room
Windrose Avenue, Scottsdale, AZ

after

the sea in a bedroom with shell-shape head- and footboards, sea blue walls, bedside shelves made from bamboo, window shades made with fabric stretched across a bamboo frame, a wide wallpaper border, and a sea-grass rug.

E44: Miami, FL: Miami Place
Cast: Paige, Hildi, Laurie, Ty

Hildi sees spots in a large living room by upholstering several pieces of furniture with cream fabric covered in white and black circles, painting the walls to match the fabric, building a circular shelving unit/entertainment center, repairing existing water damage on the walls, hanging matchstick blinds, and laying a new khaki carpet. Laurie warms a bland living room with gold paint and by creating a molding design on the ceiling, hanging a square light fixture, constructing a large built-in cabinet for the big-screen TV, creating a seating area and a dining area, and designing a Hans Hofmann-inspired painting for the new dining area.

E45: Miramar, FL: Avenue 164
Cast: Paige, Doug, Frank, Ty

Doug energizes a bland white kitchen by painting the walls citron green and the cabinets tomato red, adding concentric rectangles to the cabinet fronts with molding, replacing some drawers with dark brown wicker baskets, and adding several brightly colored plants in white pots throughout the room. Paige names Doug's room "Contempo-ribbean Kitchen." Frank looks to the future in a bedroom by painting the walls deep red, building a headboard out of various upholstered shapes, sewing a duvet cover from vintage fabric, painting the existing furniture black, hanging long black doors around the room as artwork, and designing a large black futuristically styled entertainment center.

▶after

Edward's Room
Seventh Street, Los Angeles, CA

E46: Orlando, FL: Smith Street
Cast: Paige, Hildi, Kia, Amy Wynn

Hildi helps reorganize the space in an efficiency apartment by painting the walls yellow, building a large bed unit that can be used as a king-size bed or divided so the homeowner's daughter has her own space when she visits, making a roll screen from her own photo of the Arc d'Triumph to divide the bed, adding a dining/entertaining area with thrift store tables and chairs, reconfiguring the closet storage to include a desk area, and painting the carpet brown. Kia remakes a bedroom in a Moroccan theme, painting the walls green, hanging purple, green, and gold draperies; adding a copper glaze to the ceiling; installing a ceiling fan; building a large headboard with a Moroccan-motif cutout; hanging wallpaper "columns" on the wall; and replacing the existing closet doors with mirrored ones.

E47: Florida: Night Owl Lane
Cast: Paige, Edward, Hildi, Amy Wynn

Edward adds Eastern flair to a bedroom by painting the walls yellow; designing a headboard with decoratively framed bulletin boards and a footboard with stylized feet; installing two bedside tables mounted to the wall; painting a piece of custom artwork of a Buddha image; antiquing a thrift store dresser, mirror, and bench; hanging brown fabric on the windows; and hanging white curtains stenciled with brown henna-style markings to disguise the dressing area. Hildi streamlines a large art collection by building a new wall with several large shelves to display paintings, texturing the walls with stucco, laying a parquet floor, and changing the furniture configuration.

E48: Los Angeles, CA: Elm Street (Celebrity Episode)
Cast: Paige, Genevieve, Vern, Ty

Gen updates Sarah Rue's office by painting the walls smoky taupe and the trim brown, building a mahogany L-shape corner desk out of two doors and two oxidized filing cabinets, designing a banquette/lounge seating area, adding red decorative accents, and displaying framed line drawings of cats created by her team. Vern adds warmth to Andy Dick's kitchen and breakfast nook by painting the walls two different shades of terra-cotta, installing a faux-terra-cotta tile floor and a brown tile countertop, adding wrought-iron hardware and decorative accents, painting a graphic circular image across several canvases, and sewing rust-tone Roman shades.

E49: Santa Monica, CA: Ocean Park
Cast: Paige, Laurie, Vern, Ty

Laurie unifies a living room by painting the walls yellow, adding a ready-made desk, hanging Gottlieb-inspired paintings on either side of the fireplace, building out the existing fireplace with a new mantel, laying a new area rug, installing wall shelves, and adding horseshoe-shape

chairs. Vern designs a meditative look in a bedroom by painting the walls light blue, building a large white headboard with a square inset shelf to hold a Buddha statue, installing a large entertainment center/shelving unit, adding two bedside tables, and hanging a silver-leaf candle shelf.

E50: Los Angeles, CA: Irving Street
Cast: Paige, Frank, Genevieve, Ty

Frank adds a modern twist to a bachelor's living room by painting the walls sky blue, adding black and taupe paint to the fireplace, buying all new furniture and lamps, building a wood bar, framing a black and white string art project, and hanging several of the homeowner's photos. Gen looks to orchids for color inspiration in a living room and paints the walls white and the trim green, installs green molding on the curved ceiling, builds a low-slung sofa and a new dining table, and hangs three line drawings of orchids.

E51: California: Via Jardin
Cast: Paige, Laurie, Vern, Amy Wynn

Laurie warms up a living room by painting the walls orange, painting large bookshelves with black and red lacquer, building a vertical fireplace extension with an octagon motif made from decorative molding, creating a bamboo-framed full-length mirror, slipcovering the furniture with white fabric, and accenting a long wall with a row of white vertical rectangles made from molding. Vern softens the colors in a kitchen by painting the "slaughterhouse red" walls yellow-cream, expanding the island top, designing a seating bench with inside storage, turning a tall bookcase on its side to become a bench/shoe storage area, hanging stainless-steel pot shelving above the stove, and laying new wood laminate flooring.

E52: Los Angeles, CA: Seventh Street (Celebrity Episode)
Cast: Paige, Edward, Hildi, Amy Wynn

Edward gets funky in Beverly Mitchell's garage rec room by painting the walls gray; building room screens that are painted gray and chartreuse; upholstering thrift store and existing furniture with chartreuse fabric; building a bar area; hanging white, gray, and chartreuse curtains on rods made of bent pipe to hide the laundry area; and hanging paper lanterns over the seating area. Hildi brings a little refinement to George and Jeff Stoltz's bachelor pad living room by covering the walls with blue faux suede, laying a khaki carpet, building a large armoire with woven raffia doors, installing a small wall near the front door to create a short hallway, reupholstering two thrift store sofas, building a small bar-style table, hanging a bike spray-painted silver on the wall as sculpture, and framing black and white photos of Hildi's and her team's tummies.

E53: Orlando, FL: Winter Song Drive
Cast: Paige, Doug, Vern, Ty

Doug gives an enclosed patio a martini bar look by painting

after

the walls white, adding a marble tile top to an existing bar, covering the front of the bar with aluminum flashing, mounting a TV on the wall, hanging multiple white waterproof curtains, using silver conduit as a drapery rod, building banquette and upholstered cube seating, and attaching several round automotive mirrors to the wall. Vern gives new life to a living room by painting three walls taupe and one wall rust red, laying a new sea-grass rug, painting the existing armoire tan and the side tables rust-red, building an upholstered removable top for the coffee table so it can double as an ottoman, and buying a brown sectional sofa from a thrift store.

E54: Orlando, FL: Whisper Lake
Cast: Paige, Frank, Hildi, Amy Wynn
Frank lightens a family room by dry-brushing the walls with white paint and the wainscoting with sage green paint, adding a broken tile mosaic to the existing fireplace, hanging fishnetting as a valance, upholstering the existing furniture with sage green fabric, painting the existing armoire pale blue, and installing lighthouse-themed hardware on the armoire doors and drawers. Hildi spices up a living room by painting the walls red, upholstering the furniture in and making draperies from cream fabric printed with red Asian-themed designs, building a new wall to better define the space, demolishing a small half-wall, transforming wicker chicken cages into light fixtures, and painting the coffee and side tables black.

E55: South Carolina: Innisbrook Lane
Cast: Paige, Frank, Laurie, Carter
Frank brightens a large living room by painting the walls yellow, decoupaging green and white marbled paper to insets on the fireplace, hanging navy blue drapes, slipcovering the furniture in both red and taupe fabric, laying a large natural-tone rug, and covering the bases of two new lamps with the same paper used on the fireplace. Laurie revamps a living room with a color

palette inspired by a van Gogh print. Three walls are painted sage green; the remaining wall is painted with horizontal stripes in sage green, olive green, yellow, and white; a new silver light fixture is hung; the furniture is rearranged into a more comfortable conversation area; doors are added to the existing armoire; and a large square fabric-topped coffee table is built complete with four large storage drawers.

E56: South Carolina: Sherborne Drive
Cast: Paige, Doug, Edward, Carter
Doug creates a comfortable modern den by painting the walls dark plum-gray, laying a dark gray carpet, covering the ceiling with draped sheets of white poster board, installing a long L-shape banquette seating area with circular supports, building upholstered stools, hanging canvases and adding tufted pillows in light lavender shades, and creating a half-wall with strips of wood woven through pipe supports. Edward adds a modern twist to Moroccan style in a living room by painting the ceiling teal, texturing two of the walls with crumpled tissue paper, painting the walls mustard yellow, covering the brick fireplace with terra-cotta-tinted cement, building a large mantel spray-painted to look like stone, and adding wrought-iron decorative accents.

E57: Pennsylvania: Tremont Drive
Cast: Paige, Genevieve, Vern, Amy Wynn
Gen kick-starts a boy's bedroom by painting the walls bright green, adding a black and white racing stripe around the room on the center of the walls, building a raised platform for the bed and desk, creating a seating area with a green rug and orange chairs, suspending several green and white paper lanterns above the bed, and adding multiple pieces of hockey memorabilia around the room. Vern designs an inviting living room by painting the walls gold, applying copper leaf to a large inset in the ceiling, slipcovering an existing and a thrift

store sofa in brown velvet, building a chaise lounge, tiling the top of the existing coffee table with brown and gold glass tiles, and creating a large burgundy cabinet/bar wall unit by mixing ready-made and newly constructed pieces.

E58: Pennsylvania: Bryant Court
Cast: Paige, Hildi, Laurie, Amy Wynn
Hildi makes a bold statement in a dining room by painting the walls and ceiling black, painting a thrift store table and chairs bright golden yellow, installing a large black light fixture that holds 53 exposed lightbulbs, hanging cream draperies, upholstering the dining chairs with twig-print cream fabric, hanging metal screens spray-painted chrome on the wall, and creating several flower arrangements in vases filled with boiled eggs. Laurie pumps up the pizzazz in a room shared by two little girls by painting the walls bright green, hand painting large pink and yellow zinnias across the walls, building square headboards upholstered in pink and yellow plaid fabric, creating two new toy boxes painted with each girl's initials, painting the existing furniture and trim yellow, and creating a small tea table area. She names the room "Zany for Zinnias."

E59: Pennsylvania: Cresheim Road
Cast: Paige, Hildi, Kia, Amy Wynn
Hildi goes glam in an office by painting the walls and trim magenta, laying black foam squares as carpeting, building an 11-foot-long couch upholstered in pink python-print vinyl with white lights underneath, sewing purple sequined throw pillows, hanging magenta velvet drapes, installing a large white desk unit, and adding a magenta chair. She names the room "Mom's Lipstick Palace." Kia gets musical in a kitchen by painting the walls "turmeric yellow," painting the trim white, installing a sheet-metal backsplash, adding new cabinets and countertops, decoupaging sheet music on the top of a new island, suspending a trombone to be used as a pot rack, installing a ceiling fan, and creating a cabinet door that looks like a large bass complete with vintage accessories.

after

decorating idea index

The following lists give you all the information you need to pinpoint the *Trading Spaces* episodes that feature the room types, styles, themes, and projects you need to inspire your next room makeover.

Each listing includes the episode name, the season and episode number, and the room's designer. Dive in!

Room Types

Basement/Recreational Rooms
Washington, D.C.: Cleveland Park (S1, E7), Doug
Philadelphia, PA: Galahad Road (S1, E12), Gen
Knoxville, TN: Courtney Oak (S1, E13), Frank
Knoxville, TN: Stubbs Bluff (S1, E20), Frank
Quakertown, PA: Quakers Way (S2, E1), Hildi
New Jersey: Tall Pines Drive (S2, E2), Laurie
Philadelphia, PA: Jeannes Street (S2, E10), Gen
Chicago, IL: Fairview Avenue (S2, E16), Gen
Seattle, WA: 56th Place (S2, E23), Hildi
Los Angeles, CA: Springdale Drive (S2, E34), Laurie
New York: Half Hollow Turn (S3, E7), Kia
Los Angeles, CA: Seventh Street (S3, E52), Edward

Bathrooms
Mississippi: Golden Pond (S3, E27), Hildi

Bedrooms (Adult)
Knoxville, TN: Forest Glen (S1, E2), Doug
Knoxville, TN: Courtney Oak (S1, E13), Laurie
Cincinnati, OH: Madison & Forest (S1, E16), Laurie
San Diego, CA: Elm Ridge (S1, E17), Gen
San Diego, CA: Elm Ridge (S1, E17), Hildi
Miami, FL: 168th/83rd Streets (S1, E21), Dez
Orlando, FL: Lake Catherine (S1, E27), Hildi
Orlando, FL: Gotha Furlong (S1, E28), Gen
Orlando, FL: Gotha Furlong (S1, E28), Frank
New Orleans, LA: Walter Road (S1, E33), Gen
New York: Sherwood Drive (S1, E36), Vern
New York: Sherwood Drive (S1, E36), Doug
New Jersey: Sam Street (S1, E38), Hildi
New Jersey: Tall Pines Drive (S2, E2), Vern
Maple Glen, PA: Fiedler Road (S2, E3), Laurie
Providence, RI: Wallis Avenue (S2, E6), Gen
Boston, MA: Institute Road (S2, E9), Doug
New Jersey: Perth Road (S2, E11), Laurie
Maryland: Village Green (S2, E12), Gen
Maryland: Village Green (S2, E12), Doug

Maryland: Fairway Court (S2, E13), Vern
Maryland: Fairway Court (S2, E13), Doug
Chicago, IL: Spaulding Avenue (S2, E15), Hildi
Colorado: Stoneflower Drive (S2, E20), Frank
Seattle, WA: Dakota Street (S2, E22), Laurie
Oregon: Alyssum Avenue (S2, E24), Hildi
California: Corte Rosa (S2, E28), Vern
California: Corte Rosa (S2, E28), Laurie
California: Grenadine Way (S2, E29), Vern
Austin, TX: La Costa Drive (S2, E36), Vern
Texas: Sherwood Street (S2, E37), Gen
Houston, TX: Appalachian Trail (S2, E39), Doug
Plano, TX: Shady Valley Road (S2, E41), Hildi
Raleigh, NC: Legging Lane (S2, E43), Hildi
North Carolina: Southerby Drive (S2, E44), Doug
North Carolina: Southerby Drive (S2, E44), Hildi
Wake Forest, NC: Rodney Bay (S2, E45), Vern
Maine: Joseph Drive (S3, E3), Laurie
Maine: Joseph Drive (S3, E3), Frank
Long Island, NY: Steuben Boulevard (S3, E4), Edward
New York: Whitlock Road (S3, E6), Gen
New York: Whitlock Road (S3, E6), Doug
Philadelphia, PA: 22nd Street (S3, E8), Gen
Pennsylvania: Gorski Lane (S3, E10), Frank
Pennsylvania: Gorski Lane (S3, E10), Doug
Long Island, NY: Dover Court (S3, E11), Edward
Pennsylvania: Victoria Drive (S3, E12), Kia
New Jersey: Catania Court (S3, E15), Hildi
Virginia: Gentle Heights Court (S3, E17), Kia
Arlington, VA: First Road (S3, E18), Hildi
Arlington, VA: First Road (S3, E18), Doug
Washington, D.C.: Quebec Place (S3, E19), Vern
Indiana: Fieldhurst Lane (S3, E21), Doug
Indiana: Fieldhurst Lane (S3, E21), Vern
Indianapolis, IN: Halleck Way (S3, E22), Edward
Indianapolis, IN: Halleck Way (S3, E22), Kia
Missouri: Sunburst Drive (S3, E23), Gen
Missouri: Sunburst Drive (S3, E23), Vern
Missouri: Sweetbriar Lane (S3, E25), Edward
Missouri: Sweetbriar Lane (S3, E25), Frank
London, England: Garden Flat (S3, E26), Gen
Mississippi: Golden Pond (S3, E27), Laurie
Mississippi: Winsmere Way (S3, E28), Laurie

Mississippi: Winsmere Way (S3, E28), Hildi
San Clemente, CA: Camino Mojada (S3, E33), Gen
California: Dusty Trail (S3, E34), Doug
California: Fairfield (S3, E35), Frank
San Diego, CA: Duenda Road (S3, E36), Frank
Scottsdale, AZ: Bell Road (S3, E38), Vern
Scottsdale, AZ: Windrose Avenue (S3, E39), Doug
Scottsdale, AZ: Windrose Avenue (S3, E39), Frank
Vegas, NV: Carlsbad Caverns (S3, E40), Doug
Miami, FL: Ten Court (S3, E43), Kia
Miramar, FL: Avenue 164 (S3, E45), Frank
Orlando, FL: Smith Street (S3, E46), Kia
Florida: Night Owl Lane (S3, E47), Edward
Santa Monica, CA: Ocean Park (S3, E49), Vern

Bedrooms (Children's)
Athens, GA: County Road (S1, E3), Frank
Cincinnati, OH: Sturbridge Road (S1, E15), Gen
Orlando, FL: Winterhaven (S1, E29), Doug
New Orleans, LA: D'evereaux Street (S1, E34), Vern
Boston, MA: Ashfield Street (S2, E7), Laurie
Boston, MA: Ashfield Street (S2, E7), Gen
Long Island, NY: Dover Court (S3, E11), Vern
Virginia: Gentle Heights Court (S3, E17), Hildi
Scott Air Force Base, MO: Ash Creek (S3, E24), Doug
London, England: Garden Flat (S3, E26), Hildi
Scottsdale, AZ: Bell Road (S3, E38), Frank
Pennsylvania: Tremont Drive (S3, E57), Gen
Pennsylvania: Bryant Court (S3, E58), Laurie

Dens
Knoxville, TN: Fourth & Gill (S1, E1), Frank
Boston, MA: Institute Road (S2, E9), Frank
South Carolina: Sherborne Drive (S3, E56), Doug

Dining Rooms
Alpharetta, GA: Providence Oaks (S1, E4), Hildi
Philadelphia, PA: Valley Road (S1, E11), Laurie
Cincinnati, OH: Sturbridge Road (S1, E15), Doug
Austin, TX: Wycliff (S1, E24), Hildi
New Jersey: Sam Street (S1, E38), Laurie
California: Peralta Street (S2, E32), Doug
Los Angeles, CA: Springdale Drive (S2, E34), Vern
Long Island, NY: Steuben Boulevard (S3, E4), Frank
New Jersey: Catania Court (S3, E15), Gen
Austin, TX: Wyoming Valley Drive (S3, E30), Laurie
Pennsylvania: Bryant Court (S3, E58), Hildi

Family Rooms
Portland, OR: Everett Street (S2, E26), Doug
Orlando, FL: Whisper Lake (S3, E54), Frank

Kitchens
Knoxville, TN: Fourth & Gill (S1, E1), Laurie
Buckhead, GA: Canter Road (S1, E6), Gen
Alexandria, VA: Riefton Court (S1, E8), Frank
Annapolis, MD: Fox Hollow (S1, E9), Laurie

Cincinnati, OH: Melrose Avenue (SI, EI4), Hildi
San Diego, CA: Hermes Avenue (SI, EI8), Laurie
San Diego, CA: Wilbur Street (SI, EI9), Doug
Knoxville, TN: Stubbs Bluff (SI, E20), Doug
Fort Lauderdale, FL: 59th Street (SI, E22), Hildi
Austin, TX: Wycliff (SI, E24), Doug
Austin, TX: Wing Road (SI, E25), Gen
Orlando, FL: Lake Catherine (SI, E27), Vern
Santa Fe, NM: Felize (SI, E3I), Vern
New Orleans, LA: Jacob Street (SI, E32), Hildi
New Orleans, LA: Walter Road (SI, E33), Frank
New Jersey: Lincroft (SI, E39), Laurie
Providence, RI: Wallis Avenue (S2, E6), Frank
Chicago, IL: Edward Road (S2, EI4), Frank
Chicago, IL: Fairview Avenue (S2, EI6), Vern
Colorado: Berry Avenue (S2, EI7), Gen
Oregon: Alsea Court (S2, E25), Frank
Oakland, CA: Webster Street (S2, E3I), Gen
Texas: Sherwood Street (S2, E37), Frank
Texas: Sutton Court (S2, E42), Laurie
Maine: George Road (S3, EI), Doug
Maine: George Road (S3, EI), Gen
Long Island, NY: Split Rock Road (S3, E5), Gen
Long Island, NY: Split Rock Road (S3, E5), Vern
Philadelphia, PA: Gettysburg Lane (S3, E9), Frank
Nazareth, PA: First Street (S3, EI4), Doug
Austin, TX: Wyoming Valley Drive (S3, E30), Hildi
California: Dusty Trail (S3, E34), Gen
Miramar, FL: Avenue I64 (S3, E45), Doug
California: Via Jardin (S3, E5I), Vern
Pennsylvania: Cresheim Road (S3, E59), Kia

Living Rooms

Knoxville, TN: Forest Glen (SI, E2), Hildi
Lawrenceville, GA: Pine Lane (SI, E5), Dez
Lawrenceville, GA: Pine Lane (SI, E5), Hildi
Buckhead, GA: Canter Road (SI, E6), Laurie
Washington, D.C.: Cleveland Park (SI, E7), Dez
Alexandria, VA: Riefton Court (SI, E8), Gen
Annapolis, MD: Fox Hollow (SI, E9), Gen
Philadelphia, PA: Strathmore Road (SI, EI0), Frank
Philadelphia, PA: Strathmore Road (SI, EI0), Dez
Cincinnati, OH: Melrose Avenue (SI, EI4), Frank
Cincinnati, OH: Madison & Forest (SI, EI6), Doug
San Diego, CA: Hermes Avenue (SI, EI8), Gen
San Diego, CA: Wilbur Street (SI, EI9), Frank
Miami, FL: I68th/83rd Streets (SI, E2I), Laurie
Fort Lauderdale, FL: 59th Street (SI, E22), Frank
Key West, FL: Elizabeth Street (SI, E23), Frank
Key West, FL: Elizabeth Street (SI, E23), Gen
Austin, TX: Wing Road (SI, E25), Hildi
Austin, TX: Birdhouse Drive (SI, E26), Frank
Orlando, FL: Winterhaven (SI, E29), Laurie
Albuquerque, NM: Gloria (SI, E30), Hildi
Albuquerque, NM: Gloria (SI, E30), Doug
Santa Fe, NM: Felize (SI, E3I), Gen
New York: Shore Road (SI, E35), Dez

New York: Linda Court (SI, E37), Doug
New York: Linda Court (SI, E37), Frank
New Jersey: Lincroft (SI, E39), Doug
New Jersey: Lafayette Street (SI, E40), Vern
Quakertown, PA: Quakers Way (S2, EI), Doug
Maple Glen, PA: Fiedler Road (S2, E3), Gen
Northampton, PA: James Avenue (S2, E4), Hildi
Northampton, PA: James Avenue (S2, E4), Frank
Providence, RI: Phillips Street (S2, E5), Hildi
Providence, RI: Phillips Street (S2, E5), Vern
Springfield, MA: Sunset Terrace (S2, E8), Hildi
Springfield, MA: Sunset Terrace (S2, E8), Vern
New Jersey: Perth Road (S2, EII), Frank
Chicago, IL: Edward Road (S2, EI4), Laurie
Chicago, IL: Spaulding Avenue (S2, EI5), Doug
Colorado: Berry Avenue (S2, EI7), Hildi
Colorado: Cherry Street (S2, EI8), Gen
Colorado: Cherry Street (S2, EI8), Laurie
Colorado: Andes Way (S2, EI9), Frank
Colorado: Andes Way (S2, EI9), Vern
Colorado: Stoneflower Drive (S2, E20), Doug
Seattle, WA: I37th Street (S2, E2I), Doug
Seattle, WA: I37th Street (S2, E2I), Frank
Seattle, WA: Dakota Street (S2, E22), Vern
Seattle, WA: 56th Place (S2, E23), Gen
Oregon: Alyssum Avenue (S2, E24), Gen
Oregon: Alsea Court (S2, E25), Laurie
Santa Clara, CA: Lafayette Street (S2, E27), Frank
California: Grenadine Way (S2, E29), Frank
Oakland, CA: Webster Street (S2, E3I), Hildi
California: Peralta Street (S2, E32), Hildi
Los Angeles, CA: Willoughby Avenue (S2, E33), Doug
Los Angeles, CA: Willoughby Avenue (S2, E33), Gen
California: Abbeywood Lane (S2, E35), Frank
California: Abbeywood Lane (S2, E35), Hildi
Houston, TX: Sawdust Street (S2, E38), Laurie
Houston, TX: Sawdust Street (S2, E38), Doug
Plano, TX: Bent Horn Court (S2, E40), Vern
Texas: Sutton Court (S2, E42), Frank
Wake Forest, NC: Rodney Bay (S2, E45), Laurie
Portland, OR: Rosemont Avenue (S3, E2), Laurie
Portland, OR: Rosemont Avenue (S3, E2), Vern
New York: Half Hollow Turn (S3, E7), Frank
Philadelphia, PA: 22nd Street (S3, E8), Edward
Philadelphia, PA: Gettysburg Lane (S3, E9), Vern
Pennsylvania: Victoria Drive (S3, EI2), Doug
New Jersey: Manitoba Trail (S3, EI3), Doug
Nazareth, PA: First Street (S3, EI4), Vern
Philadelphia, PA: East Avenue (S3, EI6), Hildi
Philadelphia, PA: East Avenue (S3, EI6), Frank
Washington, D.C.: Quebec Place (S3, EI9), Gen
Indianapolis, IN: River Valley Drive (S3, E20), Gen
Indianapolis, IN: River Valley Drive (S3, E20), Doug
San Antonio, TX: Ghostbridge (S3, E29), Hildi
San Antonio, TX: Ghostbridge (S3, E29), Vern
Austin, TX: Aire Libre Drive (S3, E3I), Frank

Austin, TX: Aire Libre Drive (S3, E3I), Kia
Austin, TX: Wampton Way (S3, E32), Gen
Austin, TX: Wampton Way (S3, E32), Doug
San Diego, CA: Duenda Road (S3, E36), Vern
Los Angeles, CA: Murietta Avenue (S3, E37), Laurie
Vegas, NV: Carlsbad Caverns (S3, E40), Hildi
Vegas, NV: Smokemont Courts (S3, E4I), Laurie
Vegas, NV: Woodmoro Court (S3, E42), Gen
Vegas, NV: Woodmore Court (S3, E42), Vern
Miami, FL: Ten Court (S3, E43), Hildi
Miami, FL: Miami Place (S3, E44), Hildi
Miami, FL: Miami Place (S3, E44), Laurie
Florida: Night Owl Lane (S3, E47), Hildi
Santa Monica, CA: Ocean Park (S3, E49), Laurie
Los Angeles, CA: Irving Street (S3, E50), Frank
Los Angeles, CA: Irving Street (S3, E50), Gen
California: Via Jardin (S3, E5I), Laurie
Los Angeles, CA: Seventh Street (S3, E52), Hildi
Orlando, FL: Winter Song Drive (S3, E53), Vern
Orlando, FL: Whisper Lake (S3, E54), Hildi
South Carolina: Innisbrook Lane (S3, E55), Frank
South Carolina: Innisbrook Lane (S3, E55), Laurie
South Carolina: Sherborne Drive (S3, E56), Edward
Pennsylvania: Tremont Drive (S3, E57), Vern

Multipurpose Rooms

Athens, GA: County Road (SI, E3), Hildi
(kitchen/living room)
Alpharetta, GA: Providence Oaks (SI, E4),
Roderick (den/guest room)
Philadelphia, PA: Galahad Road (SI, EI2), Hildi
(living/dining room)
Austin, TX: Birdhouse Drive (SI, E26), Laurie
(living/dining room)
New Orleans, LA: Jacob Street (SI, E32), Laurie
(kitchen/office/dining/living room)
New Orleans, LA: D'evereaux Street (SI, E34),
Gen (den/guest room)
New Jersey: Lafayette Street (SI, E40), Frank
(dining/living room)
Portland, OR: Everett Street (S2, E26), Vern
(living/dining room)
Houston, TX: Appalachian Trail (S2, E39), Laurie
(office/playroom)
New Jersey: Manitoba Trail (S3, EI3), Frank
(living/dining room)
Scott Air Force Base, MO: Ash Creek (S3, E24),
Kia (living/dining room)
California: Fairfield (S3, E35), Kia (office/game
room)
Los Angeles, CA: Murietta Avenue (S3, E37), Gen
(living/dining room)
Orlando, FL: Smith Street (S3, E46), Hildi
(bedroom/dining room/entertaining
area/office)
Los Angeles, CA: Elm Street (S3, E48), Vern
(kitchen/breakfast nook)

New Jersey: Manitoba Trail (S3, E13), Frank
New Jersey: Catania Court (S3, E15), Hildi
Austin, TX: Aire Libre Drive (S3, E31), Kia
Austin, TX: Wampton Way (S3, E32), Doug
California: Dusty Trail (S3, E34), Gen
San Diego, CA: Duenda Road (S3, E36), Frank
San Diego, CA: Duenda Road (S3, E36), Vern
Miramar, FL: Avenue 164 (S3, E45), Doug
Orlando, FL: Smith Street (S3, E46), Kia
South Carolina: Innisbrook Lane (S3, E55), Laurie
Pennsylvania: Tremont Drive (S3, E57), Gen
Pennsylvania: Bryant Court (S3, E58), Laurie

Blues

Philadelphia, PA: Valley Road (S1, E11), Doug
Knoxville, TN: Courtney Oak (S1, E13), Frank
San Diego, CA: Hermes Avenue (S1, E18), Laurie
Key West, FL: Elizabeth Street (S1, E23), Frank
Santa Fe, NM: Felize (S1, E31), Vern
New York: Sherwood Drive (S1, E36), Vern
Quakertown, PA: Quakers Way (S2, E1), Hildi
Providence, RI: Wallis Avenue (S2, E6), Frank
Boston, MA: Ashfield Street (S2, E7), Gen
Maryland: Fairway Court (S2, E13), Doug
Oregon: Alyssum Avenue (S2, E24), Hildi
California: Grenadine Way (S2, E29), Vern
Los Angeles, CA: Willoughby Avenue (S2, E33), Gen
Houston, TX: Appalachian Trail (S2, E39), Doug
North Carolina: Southerby Drive (S2, E44), Doug
Portland, OR: Rosemont Avenue (S3, E2), Laurie
Long Island, NY: Dover Court (S3, E11), Vern
Virginia: Gentle Heights Court (S3, E17), Hildi
Arlington, VA: First Road (S3, E18), Hildi
Indiana: Fieldhurst Lane (S3, E21), Vern
Missouri: Sunburst Drive (S3, E23), Vern
California: Dusty Trail (S3, E34), Doug
Miami, FL: Ten Court (S3, E43), Hildi
Miami, FL: Ten Court (S3, E43), Kia
Santa Monica, CA: Ocean Park (S3, E49), Vern
Los Angeles, CA: Irving Street (S3, E50), Frank
Los Angeles, CA: Seventh Street (S3, E52), Hildi

Purples

Athens, GA: County Road (S1, E3), Frank
Alpharetta, GA: Providence Oaks (S1, E4), Hildi
Cincinnati, OH: Madison & Forest (S1, E16), Doug
Boston, MA: Ashfield Street (S2, E7), Laurie
Colorado: Berry Avenue (S2, E17), Gen
California: Peralta Street (S2, E32), Hildi
Raleigh, NC: Legging Lane (S2, E43), Hildi
Philadelphia, PA: East Avenue (S3, E16), Frank
Scottsdale, AZ: Bell Road (S3, E38), Frank
Scottsdale, AZ: Bell Road (S3, E38), Vern
Scottsdale, AZ: Windrose Avenue (S3, E39), Frank

Browns

Knoxville, TN: Fourth & Gill (S1, E1), Frank

Buckhead, GA: Canter Road (S1, E6), Laurie
Philadelphia, PA: Strathmore Road (S1, E10), Frank
Philadelphia, PA: Valley Road (S1, E11), Laurie
Philadelphia, PA: Galahad Road (S1, E12), Hildi
Cincinnati, OH: Melrose Avenue (S1, E14), Frank
Cincinnati, OH: Sturbridge Road (S1, E15), Doug
Knoxville, TN: Stubbs Bluff (S1, E20), Frank
Knoxville, TN: Stubbs Bluff (S1, E20), Doug
Austin, TX: Wycliff (S1, E24), Hildi
Santa Fe, NM: Felize (S1, E31), Gen
New York: Sherwood Drive (S1, E36), Doug
New Jersey: Lincroft (S1, E39), Doug
New Jersey: Tall Pines Drive (S2, E2), Vern
Boston, MA: Institute Road (S2, E9), Doug
Maryland: Village Green (S2, E12), Gen
Chicago, IL: Fairview Avenue (S2, E16), Gen
Colorado: Berry Avenue (S2, E17), Hildi
Seattle, WA: 137th Street (S2, E21), Doug
Portland, OR: Everett Street (S2, E26), Doug
Maine: George Road (S3, E1), Doug
New York: Whitlock Road (S3, E6), Gen
Pennsylvania: Victoria Drive (S3, E12), Doug
Indianapolis, IN: Halleck Way (S3, E22), Edward
Missouri: Sunburst Drive (S3, E23), Gen
Vegas, NV: Carlsbad Caverns (S3, E40), Doug
Vegas, NV: Smokemont Courts (S3, E41), Laurie

Taupes/Light Khakis

Alpharetta, GA: Providence Oaks (S1, E4), Roderick
Austin, TX: Wycliff (S1, E24), Doug
Orlando, FL: Gotha Furlong (S1, E28), Frank
New Orleans, LA: Walter Road (S1, E33), Frank
Maple Glen, PA: Fiedler Road (S2, E3) Gen
Springfield, MA: Sunset Terrace (S2, E8), Hildi
New Jersey: Perth Road (S2, E11), Frank
Colorado: Andes Way (S2, E19), Frank
Colorado: Andes Way (S2, E19), Vern
California: Corte Rosa (S2, E28), Vern
Texas: Sutton Court (S3, E42), Laurie
Long Island, NY: Steuben Boulevard (S3, E4), Edward
Nazareth, PA: First Street (S3, E14), Vern
Washington, D.C.: Quebec Place (S3, E19), Gen
San Clemente, CA: Camino Mojada (S3, E33), Gen
San Clemente, CA: Camino Mojada (S3, E33), Vern
California: Fairfield (S3, E35), Frank
Orlando, FL: Winter Song Drive (S3, E53), Vern

Blacks

San Diego, CA: Elm Ridge (S1, E17), Hildi
New Orleans, LA: D'evereaux Street (S1, E34), Vern
Austin, TX: Wyoming Valley Drive (S3, E30), Hildi
Pennsylvania: Bryant Court (S3, E58), Hildi

Grays

Knoxville, TN: Forest Glen (S1, E2), Hildi
Philadelphia, PA: Strathmore Road (S1, E10), Dez
Orlando, FL: Lake Catherine (S1, E27), Hildi

Albuquerque, NM: Gloria (S1, E30), Doug
Providence, RI: Phillips Street (S2, E5), Hildi
Maryland: Village Green (S2, E12), Doug
Maryland: Fairway Court (S2, E13), Vern
Berkeley, CA: Prospect Street (S2, E30), Gen
Wake Forest, NC: Rodney Bay (S2, E45), Vern
Arlington, VA: First Road (S3, E18), Doug
Indiana: River Valley Drive (S3, E20), Gen
Scott Air Force Base, MO: Ash Creek (S3, E24), Doug
Scott Air Force Base, MO: Ash Creek (S3, E24), Kia
Missouri: Sweetbriar Lane (S3, E25), Edward
Vegas, NV: Smokemont Courts (S3, E41), Edward
Los Angeles, CA: Elm Street (S3, E48), Gen
Los Angeles, CA: Seventh Street (S3, E52), Edward
South Carolina: Sherborne Drive (S3, E56), Doug

Whites & Off-Whites

Athens, GA: County Road (S1, E3), Hildi
Lawrenceville, GA: Pine Lane (S1, E5), Dez
Lawrenceville, GA: Pine Lane (S1, E5), Hildi
Fort Lauderdale, FL: 59th Street (S1, E22), Hildi
New Orleans, LA: Jacob Street (S1, E32), Hildi
Philadelphia, PA: Jeannes Street (S2, E10), Gen
Chicago, IL: Spaulding Avenue (S2, E15), Hildi
Seattle, WA: Dakota Street (S2, E22), Laurie
Texas: Sherwood Street (S2, E37), Gen
Plano, TX: Bent Horn Court (S2, E40), Gen
Plano, TX: Bent Horn Court (S2, E40), Vern
Plano, TX: Shady Valley Road (S2, E41), Hildi
Raleigh, NC: Legging Lane (S2, E43), Frank
Philadelphia, PA: 22nd Street (S3, E8), Gen
New Jersey: Manitoba Trail (S3, E13), Doug
Nazareth, PA: First Street (S3, E14), Doug
London, England: Garden Flat (S3, E26), Hildi
San Antonio, TX: Ghostbridge (S3, E29), Hildi
Miami, FL: Miami Place (S3, E44), Hildi
Florida: Night Owl Lane (S3, E47), Hildi
Los Angeles, CA: Irving Street (S3, E50), Gen
Orlando, FL: Winter Song Drive (S3, E53), Doug
Orlando, FL: Whisper Lake (S3, E54), Frank

Themed Rooms

New Orleans, LA: D'evereaux Street
    (S1, E34), Vern; Soccer
Boston, MA: Ashfield Street (S2, E7),
    Gen; Moroccan
Philadelphia, PA: Jeannes Street (S2, E10), Gen;
    Scrabble Board
Maryland: Fairway Court (S2, E13), Doug;
    Pullman Car
Colorado: Andes Way (S2, E19), Vern; Stripes

Orlando, FL: Winterhaven (SI, E29), Doug
Albuquerque, NM: Gloria (SI, E30), Doug
Providence, RI: Phillips Street (S2, E5), Vern
Philadelphia, PA: Jeannes Street (S2, EIO), Vern
Maryland: Village Green (S2, EI2), Gen
Maryland: Fairway Court (S2, EI3), Doug
Chicago, IL: Fairview Avenue (S2, EI6), Gen
Oregon: Alsea Court (S2, E25), Frank
Santa Clara, CA: Lafayette Street (S2, E27), Frank
Oakland, CA: Webster Street (S2, E31), Hildi
Plano, TX: Shady Valley Road (S2, E4I), Doug
Portland, OR: Rosemont Avenue (S3, E2), Vern
Pennsylvania: Gorski Lane (S3, EIO), Frank
Pennsylvania: Gorski Lane (S3, EIO), Doug
New Jersey: Catania Court (S3, EI5), Hildi
California: Dusty Trail (S3, E34), Doug
California: Dusty Trail (S3, E34), Gen
Scottsdale, AZ: Bell Road (S3, E38), Vern
South Carolina: Sherborne Drive (S3, E56), Doug
Pennsylvania: Tremont Drive (S3, E57), Vern

Room Styles

Casual Rooms

Alpharetta, GA: Providence Oaks (SI, E4), Roderick
Lawrenceville, GA: Pine Lane (SI, E5), Hildi
Washington, D.C.: Cleveland Park (SI, E7), Doug
Philadelphia, PA: Valley Road (SI, EII), Doug
Philadelphia, PA: Galahad Road (SI, EI2), Gen
Knoxville, TN: Courtney Oak (SI, EI3), Frank
Knoxville, TN: Stubbs Bluff (SI, E20), Frank
Key West, FL: Elizabeth Street (SI, E23), Frank
Santa Fe, NM: Felize (SI, E31), Gen
New Orleans, LA: D'evereaux Street (SI, E34), Gen
New Jersey: Tall Pines Drive (S2, E2), Laurie
Boston, MA: Institute Road (S2, E9), Frank
Philadelphia, PA: Jeannes Street (S2, EIO), Gen
Chicago, IL: Fairview Avenue (S2, EI6), Gen
Oregon: Alsea Court (S2, E25), Frank
Berkeley, CA: Prospect Street (S2, E30), Doug
Los Angeles, CA: Willoughby Avenue (S2, E33), Gen
Plano, TX: Bent Horn Court (S2, E40), Gen
Plano, TX: Shady Valley Road (S2, E4I), Doug
Raleigh, NC: Legging Lane (S2, E43), Frank
New York: Half Hollow Turn (S3, E7), Kia
New Jersey: Manitoba Trail (S3, EI3), Frank
California: Fairfield (S3, E35), Kia
Los Angeles, CA: Elm Street (S3, E48), Gen
Los Angeles, CA: Irving Street (S3, E50), Gen
Los Angeles, CA: Seventh Street (S3, E52), Edward
Orlando, FL: Winter Song Drive (S3, E53), Doug

Orlando, FL: Winter Song Drive (S3, E53), Vern
South Carolina: Sherborne Drive (S3, E56), Edward

Formal Rooms

Alpharetta, GA: Providence Oaks (SI, E4), Hildi
Buckhead, GA: Canter Road (SI, E6), Laurie
Philadelphia, PA: Valley Road (SI, EII), Laurie
Miami, FL: I68th/03rd Streets (SI, E2I), Laurie
Austin, TX: Wing Road (SI, E25), Hildi
Austin, TX: Birdhouse Drive (SI, E26), Laurie
Maple Glen, PA: Fiedler Road (S2, E3), Gen
Springfield, MA: Sunset Terrace (S2, E8), Hildi
Springfield, MA: Sunset Terrace (S2, E8), Vern
Philadelphia, PA: Jeannes Street (S2, EIO), Vern
Colorado: Berry Avenue (S2, EI7), Hildi
California: Peralta Street (S2, E32), Doug
Los Angeles, CA: Springdale Drive (S2, E34), Vern
Wake Forest, NC: Rodney Bay (S2, E45), Laurie
New Jersey: Manitoba Trail (S3, EI3), Doug
Mississippi: Golden Pond (S3, E27), Laurie
San Antonio, TX: Ghostbridge (S3, E29), Vern
Vegas, NV: Smokemont Court (S3, E4I), Laurie
South Carolina: Innisbrook Lane (S3, E55), Laurie
Pennsylvania: Tremont Drive (S3, E57), Vern
Pennsylvania: Bryant Court (S3, E58), Hildi

Chic & Modern Rooms

Philadelphia, PA: Strathmore Road (SI, EIO), Dez
Cincinnati, OH: Madison & Forest (SI, EI6), Doug
San Diego, CA: Elm Ridge (SI, EI7), Hildi
Albuquerque, NM: Gloria (SI, E30), Doug
New Orleans, LA: Jacob Street (SI, E32), Hildi
New Orleans, LA: D'evereaux Street (SI, E34), Vern
Quakertown, PA: Quakers Way (S2, EI), Hildi
Providence, RI: Phillips Street (S2, E5), Hildi
Maryland: Village Green (S2, EI2), Doug
Colorado: Cherry Street (S2, EI8), Laurie [Well,
   it's mod, anyway.]
California: Peralta Street (S2, E32), Hildi
Los Angeles, CA: Willoughby Avenue (S2, E33), Doug
California: Abbeywood Lane (S2, E35), Hildi
Philadelphia, PA: East Avenue (S3, EI6), Hildi
Scottsdale, AZ: Bell Road (S3, E38), Vern
Vegas, NV: Smokemont Courts (S3, E4I), Edward
Miami, FL: Ten Court (S3, E43), Hildi
Miramar, FL: Avenue I64 (S3, E45), Frank
Los Angeles, CA: Irving Street (S3, E50), Frank
South Carolina: Sherborne Drive (S3, E56), Doug
Pennsylvania: Tremont Drive (S3, E57), Gen
Pennsylvania: Bryant Court (S3, E58), Hildi
Pennsylvania: Cresheim Road (S3, E59), Hildi

Cottage/Country Rooms

Knoxville, TN: Fourth & Gill (SI, EI), Frank
Knoxville, TN: Forest Glen (SI, E2), Doug
Athens, GA: County Road (SI, E3), Frank
Lawrenceville, GA: Pine Lane (SI, E5), Hildi

Lawrenceville, GA: Pine Lane (SI, E5), Dez
Alexandria, VA: Riefton Court (SI, E8), Frank
Philadelphia, PA: Valley Road (SI, EII), Doug
Knoxville, TN: Courtney Oak (SI, EI3), Frank
Cincinnati, OH: Melrose Avenue (SI, EI4), Hildi
San Diego, CA: Elm Ridge (SI, EI7), Gen
Knoxville, TN: Stubbs Bluff (SI, E20), Doug
Key West, FL: Elizabeth Street (SI, E23), Gen
Key West, FL: Elizabeth Street (SI, E23), Frank
Orlando, FL: Winterhaven (SI, E29), Doug
New Jersey: Lincroft (SI, E39), Doug
New Jersey: Lincroft (SI, E39), Laurie
New Jersey: Lafayette Street (SI, E40), Frank
Northampton, PA: James Avenue (S2, E4), Frank
Providence, RI: Wallis Avenue (S2, E6), Frank
New Jersey: Perth Road (S2, EII), Frank
Chicago, IL: Edward Road (S2, EI4), Laurie
Seattle, WA: I37th Street (S2, E2I), Doug
Seattle, WA: I37th Street (S2, E2I), Frank
Santa Clara, CA: Lafayette Street (S2, E27), Frank
Maine: George Road (S3, EI), Gen
Long Island, NY: Steuben Boulevard (S3, E4), Frank
Philadelphia, PA: Gettysburg Lane (S3, E9), Frank
New Jersey: Manitoba Trail (S3, EI3), Frank

Exotic Rooms

California: Corte Rosa (S2, E28), Vern
California: Grenadine Way (S2, E29), Vern
Pennsylvania: Gorski Lane (S3, EIO), Doug
Indianapolis, IN: Halleck Way (S3, E22), Kia
Missouri: Sunburst Drive (S3, E23), Gen
San Clemente, CA: Camino Mojada (S3, E33), Gen
Scottsdale, AZ: Windrose Avenue (S3, E39), Frank
Miami, FL: Ten Court (S3, E43), Kia
Orlando, FL: Smith Street (S3, E46), Kia
Florida: Night Owl Lane (S3, E47), Edward

Lizard Love
One homeowner
holds a large lizard
and hands it to Paige
as he leaves to go to
the other home.
(California: Via
Jardin, Season 3,
Episode 5I)